ENCOURAGEMENT
FOR THOSE WHO
SUFFER IN SILENCE
SUFFERING IN SILENCE

REV. DR. LaRUTH E. LOCKHART

WESTBOW PRESS®
A DIVISION OF THOMAS NELSON
& ZONDERVAN

Copyright © 2024 Rev. Dr. LaRuth E. Lockhart.

All rights reserved. No part of this book may be used or reproduced by any means, graphic, electronic, or mechanical, including photocopying, recording, taping or by any information storage retrieval system without the written permission of the author except in the case of brief quotations embodied in critical articles and reviews.

This book is a work of non-fiction. Unless otherwise noted, the author and the publisher make no explicit guarantees as to the accuracy of the information contained in this book and in some cases, names of people and places have been altered to protect their privacy.

WestBow Press books may be ordered through booksellers or by contacting:

WestBow Press
A Division of Thomas Nelson & Zondervan
1663 Liberty Drive
Bloomington, IN 47403
www.westbowpress.com
844-714-3454

Because of the dynamic nature of the Internet, any web addresses or links contained in this book may have changed since publication and may no longer be valid. The views expressed in this work are solely those of the author and do not necessarily reflect the views of the publisher, and the publisher hereby disclaims any responsibility for them.

Any people depicted in stock imagery provided by Getty Images are models, and such images are being used for illustrative purposes only. Certain stock imagery © Getty Images.

Cover Graphics/Art Credit: Roxie Fields

All Scripture quotations are taken from the King James Version, public domain.

ISBN: 979-8-3850-1964-9 (sc)
ISBN: 979-8-3850-1965-6 (hc)
ISBN: 979-8-3850-1966-3 (e)

Library of Congress Control Number: 2024903595

Print information available on the last page.

WestBow Press rev. date: 3/11/2024

This book is dedicated, in loving memory of my son, my mother, my grand-parents, and my prayer partners, Rev. Brenda Jenkins, Sister Barbara May, and Rev. Sandra Simmons.

Special thanks to my supporters: my husband, Rev. Benjamin Lockhart Jr., my daughter, Sharon D. Fordham, my spiritual daughter, Clara Davis, Elder Lewis L. Cole Jr., Rev. Mark S. Mayberry, Rev. Debirley Porter, and Rev. Dr. Darryl W. Robinson.

A Short Abstract/Precis

It's Time to Let Go and Let God![1]

How long will we hold on to our hidden and silent life issues? How long will we internalize our doubts and fears, our failures and unforgiveness, our pain and brokenness? Has holding on to any painful issue added anything to your life? It's time! It's time to let go and let God heal and mend what is broken in you. There is a right time for everything. God is a timely God. He's sooner than afterwhile and quicker than right now. He will hear you when you call and come to your rescue. Don't be contumacious/stubborn. Take refuge in the grace, mercy, love, and power of Almighty God. He is waiting to hear from you. We can only become whole when we give God control of every aspect of our lives—the good, the bad, and the ugly. If it had not been for the stormy issues in my life, I would not be the woman of faith that I am today. God was at His best when He delivered the Israelites from Pharaoh's army. God was at His best when He delivered Daniel and the Hebrew boys. God was at His best when He raised Lazarus from the dead. He was at His best when He healed the woman with the issue of blood. God was at His best when He sent Jesus to save me from the pit of hell, rescued me from my enemies, and delivered me from my silent issues. Let God demonstrate His best in your life. The time is now to let go and let God.

To God be all the glory!

Contents

Introduction to Suffering in Silence xi

Section 1: The Great Cover-Up

Take Off Your Mask 1
Surviving Sexual Abuse 8

Section 2: Forgiveness and Love

Forgive Like Jesus Did (LJD) 23
I Wish Jesus Hadn't Said That 33

Section 3: Inner Conflict

Chains That Bind 43
The War Within 51

Section 4: My Enemy Is Me

When You Caused the Storm 61
Three Hard Words: "I Was Wrong" 67

Section 5: Lord, Help Me

Coping with Grief and Loss 77
Coping with Health Issues 85

Section 6: Overcoming Failure

I've Failed 95
Don't Look Back 101

Epilogue: Burdens Down 107

Appendix A. Letter of Invitation to Survey Group 119
Appendix B. Survey Questionnaire/Information Gathering 121
Appendix C. Survey Results 123

Complete Notes 127
Bibliography 131

Introduction to Suffering in Silence

Upon my entrance into the world, I was told by my grandmothers that I was peculiar. As a child, I didn't understand what they meant. I pondered, *Do I look weird? Am I ugly or what?* From infancy into my late teens, they kept me in church, prayed for me, laid hands on me, and oiled me down. In the midst of all this, they were constantly saying God had me and I was going to be a preacher woman.

I was blessed to know my maternal and paternal grandparents, great-grand parents, and great-great aunts and uncles. Throughout the progression into my teens, there were always four or five generations of family members. They were all regular church attenders, which included Baptist, Methodist, and Pentecostal denominations. The family consisted of several preachers, Bible school teachers, gospel singers, and deacons.

Throughout my childhood, I witnessed my elders praising and praying to the Lord. I listened attentively as they gave words of encouragement to family and friends in times of trouble. I also witnessed how they handled or didn't handle their own difficult times of pain. Often I would kneel beside my grandma as she prayed, and from the tears and pain on her face, there appeared to be some hidden issues that were not expressed in my presence. But my grandma was a strong woman of God and surely she didn't have any unresolved issues. She couldn't be holding on to stuff, suffering in silence. Or could she?

As I continued on my life's journey and as my own storm clouds arose, I began to realize that there were some painful, heart-wrenching issues that I had pushed down deep into my inner being. I suppressed those things that I didn't want to face and wouldn't allow to surface. Discussing these things openly or even privately talking to God was not an option I considered.

I was often told by others that I was strong just like my grandma and just like her I held on to stuff. I would put up a front and put on a mask so no one could see the pain on this strong preacher woman's face.

To fill the void after a bitter divorce, my friend asked me to enroll in a Biblical Counseling class. The first class, BC-1 Self-Confrontation, was structured to teach you how to examine yourself biblically so you can live in a manner that is pleasing to God and help others do the same.[1] The students in the class were from all walks of life, including spiritual leaders and laypeople. One of the requirements of the class was to prepare a "self-confrontation testimony" addressing one of your deep-seated issues according to God's Word. The instructor would periodically inquire as to our progress with our testimonies. Students would share the ideas they planned to use as the focus of their issues. Boy, did they have some stuff to confront. I didn't have anything as serious as theirs. They had some real problems. My minor concern of losing weight was nothing in comparison to some of the major challenges they had to face. This Bible-toting preacher lady didn't have any real significant problems. Little did I know or realize that my weight issue was a *real* weight issue. I, for real, needed to do the Hebrews 12:1 "lay aside every weight."[2] By the time the Holy Spirit guided me to my self-confrontation testimony, I had cried and prayed, prayed, and cried. I began to diet and lose the heavy load of weight I carried for years, loads that I carried and suffered in silence.

This class openly revealed to me how we, as a people, even God's servants and undershepherds, suffer silently with unresolved issues. We all, if we are honest, pull wagons filled with deep-seated issues. We limp along in life with burdens we were never meant to carry. "We can't get rid of our limp until we eliminate the aggravated problem."[3] As we travel life's highway, it is to our advantage to lighten our load so that we will be free to reach our full potential in the service of our Lord. God sees all that's in our wagons of silent suffering, and He is just waiting for us to unload them at His feet.

Using my experience of suffering silently and with the Word of God as my source, I pray that this dissertation will be a blessing to others and used as resource material for my fellow silent sufferers. God has blessed me to be a blessing. I only want to pay it forward.

> "Blessed be God, even the Father of our Lord Jesus Christ, the Father of mercies, and the God of all comfort; Who comforteth us in all our tribulation, that we may be able to comfort them which are in any trouble, by the comfort wherewith we ourselves are comforted of God."[4]

We can't receive comfort until we face and admit what ails us. We must let go and let God have control of every aspect of our lives. He is the God of all healing, comfort, and restoration.

Notes

1. Broger, John C. *Self-Confrontation: A Manual for In-Depth Discipleship,* CA, Biblical Counseling Foundation (BFC), 1991.
2. Unknown. The Holy Bible (KJV), Hebrews 12:1, Nashville, TN, Broadman and Holman, 1996.
3. Fisher, James, MD. Office visit, patient-physician conversation, Marietta, GA, Fisher-Lockhart, 2021.
4. Apostle Paul. The Holy Bible KJV, 2 Corinthians 1:3–4, Nashville, TN, Broadman and Holman, 1996.

SECTION 1
THE GREAT COVER-UP

Take Off Your Mask

"The Lord is my light and my salvation; Whom shall I fear?"
—Psalm 27:1 (KJV)

A mask is defined as an object normally worn on the face. It is typically for protection, disguise, performance, or entertainment. Masks have been used since antiquity for both ceremonial and practical purposes, as well as the performing arts and entertainment.[5] The Latin word for *mask* is *persona,* which literally indicates a "false face"—a part of the personality shown to others or perceived by others.[6]

Masks have a shrewd quality about them. They are used for more than theatrical props, parts of a custom, entertainment, or protection. Masks conceal real expressions and feelings. Masks allow us to hide from others while in full view. The masked self, the false face, is the one we present to friends and family.

In the character of humans, there has always been a sense of imperfection yet a longing for perfection. Since perfection can't be attained here on earth, we try to avoid our imperfections by covering them up with masks. Many of us wear masks or facades every day. I'm not referring to the masks we wear to prevent the spread of COVID-19. We wear invisible masks to hide feelings and issues buried way down deep inside us. We put on masks to fit our needs. At work, we may put on a mask of authority and power in order to give the appearance of control. At home we wear the mask of contentment ("Everything is OK") out of fear that our spouse may not love someone with issues. At church we wear masks of self-righteousness and pride, a mask of "I've got this God thing under control; I don't need any help." Some church folk take off their Sunday go-to-meeting mask when certain people are around so they can fit in with the crowd. We shuffle our masks on and off from one situation to another.

It appears to me that we try to portray ourselves as two individuals: one without masks and one with masks. We wrestle with the self, which may or may not be under a disguise. Many of us are plagued by imposter syndrome, the fear that the world is going to find us out.[7] Guilt and shame send us into hiding behind masks. We are afraid of revealing our past, our failures, our shortcomings, our hidden issues, and the cracks in the makeup of our earthen jars.

A noted poet describes our plight in his poem "We Wear the Mask," from *The Complete Poems of Paul Laurence Dunbar*.

We Wear the Mask[8]

> We wear the mask that grins and lies, it hides our cheeks and shades our eyes,
> this debt we pay to human guile; with torn and bleeding hearts we smile
> and mouth with myriad subtleties,
> Why should the world be over-wise, in counting all our tears and sighs? Nay, let them only see us, while we wear the mask.
> We smile, but oh great Christ, our cries to thee from tortured souls arise.
> We sing, but oh the clay is vile beneath our feet, and long the mile,
> but let the world dream otherwise, we wear the mask!

God knows us inside and out. From the time of Adam and Eve, our ancestral parents, we've continued the practice of hiding and covering up as we call ourselves holy people of God. God's people aren't phony; they are real. Here is my description of God's real people:

- R: redeemed and restored
- E: empowered by the Holy Spirit

- A: acknowledgers of the Almighty God
- L: love practitioners of God and His people

However, as *real* people, we continue to wear masks. We convey the impression that we are secure, that confidence is our name and coolness is our game. We transmit vibes that our waters are calm and we are in control. But beneath the seemingly smooth surface, we are confused, wounded, and fearful souls; you and I are hiding behind masks. We are not honest with ourselves or with God.

In one of the countless famous quotes coined by William Shakespeare, in act 1, scene 3, of the famous play *Hamlet*, the character Polonius says, "This above all: to thine own self be true and it must follow, as the night the day. Thou canst not then be false to any man." To me, this means that there must be honesty and authenticity at all times, and we must make a continuous effort to demonstrate these qualities. Before Shakespeare, in God's inspired Word, Jesus said, "Why do you look at the speck of sawdust in your brother's eye and pay no attention to the plank in your own eye? How can you say to your brother, 'Let me take the speck out of your eye,' when all the time there is a plank in your own eye?"[9] Before we offer support/assistance to others, we need to confront the failures and shortcomings in our own lives from God's point of view and learn how to put off our old nature and replace it with the new nature. With our false, phony character, we enter God's house wearing our masks of anger, jealousy, fear, unforgiveness, bitterness, hatred, depression, grief, and loss as we so faithfully fulfill our ministry duties. As servants of God, we must be honest. The hierarchy of honesty is God, self, and others. When we are not honest with ourselves and God, this hinders our communication with Him and others. If we are living a concealed life, how can we get our brokenness mended? How can we receive the grace and mercy that God offers in our time of need?

No matter how proficient we become at wearing masks to fit our needs, eventually, in this life, they will become cumbersome. They may even break into pieces due to their excessive and constant changing. When this occurs, the real you may be exposed to others, as well as your recognition of who you really are.

We must understand that with God nothing is hidden, and all secrets will be known. There is nothing covered up that will not be revealed. So why do we wear masks in the presence of our omnipotent, omnipresent, omniscient God? We are the ones with the masks, not God. God can see beneath, beyond, over, above, and behind our hidden facades and false faces. God really does know our hearts, including every atrium, ventricle, and cardiac vessel. He knows what flows in and what flows out. God knows the real you.

Are you weary and heavy-laden with the burden of your masks? Disrobe now! Take them off! Take them all off! Take off your masks! Give them to God. Through prayer, we can communicate directly to Him. We won't be placed on hold. There are no phone options when we call (e.g., "Press 1 for request, press 2 for praise, press 3 for complaints, or press 4 for all other inquires."). There are no recordings that say, "Please leave a message, be blessed, and have a great day." We have a direct line to the throne of God's grace and mercy. I urge you to remove your masks, pour out your heart to God, your heavenly Father, and cast all your cares and anxieties on Him. You've had your masks a long time, so it will take time to remove them all. But you will never get them off if you don't start today. The longer you wear your masks, the tighter they fit and the harder it is to remove them. Facing your true self will be difficult. It takes courage to look at yourself in the mirror and see the real you, but you can do it with the help of the Holy Spirit. Jesus extends an invitation when He says, "Come unto me, all ye that labour and are heavy-laden, and I will give you rest. Take my yoke upon you, and learn of me; for I am meek and lowly in heart: and ye shall find rest unto your souls." (Matthew 11:28–29 KJV)

Conclusion

Learning to bare our true feelings and thoughts is vital to understanding and helping one another. Expectations are clarified and problems are solved when we courageously take off masks that hide the real self. We wear masks throughout life. Some don't realize that they have masks on.

Then some of us keep our masks on so tightly that we are afraid to remove them for we aren't certain what or whom we may find beneath the surface.

Taking off masks is like peeling onions layer by layer. We may have to shed some tears. We will peel down into the very depths of our integrity, to radical honesty about ourselves. We must commit to uncovering and knowing the truth about Mr. and Ms. Self. Disguises will only conceal who we really are and obscure the truth that makes us whole, holy, and free. As fellow mask-wearers, we can offer encouragement by being real and honest with one another. It is easy to be honest about facts; however, it's much harder to be honest about feelings and emotions. We must not let fear stop us from being true to ourselves. Remember 1 Timothy 1:7, "God did not give us a spirit of fear, but of power, and of love and of a sound mind."

With the mirror of truth (the Holy Bible) open in front of you, will you pick it up and examine yourself, looking deep into yourself? Is that a mask you see? Are you being honest with yourself, with others, with God? Honesty is where healing begins, allowing truth and light to triumph. Serenity, wisdom, peace, and the true light dissipate when honesty vanishes. Look into God's mirror. Do you know who you are? Who do you see today? Who do others see? Who does God see?

You don't have to be weighed down by your masks. You must disrobe. Take them off! Take them all off! Take off the masks and let the real *you* come forth. The masks we hide behind isolate us from the truth. In hiding the truth about ourselves, we impede our growth and wholesome communications with God and others. We would indeed be relieved of the heavy burden of trying to be who we are not when we unmask. When faced, "the truth will set you free." As the unmasked self comes in full view, new life will begin. You will live with yourself, mask on or mask off. The choice is yours.

Myself[10]

I have to live with myself and so
I want to be fit for myself to know.
I want to be able as days go by,
always to look myself straight in the eye;

I don't want to stand with the setting sun
and hate myself for the things I have done.
I don't want to keep on a closet shelf
a lot of secrets about myself
and fool myself as I come and go
into thinking no one else will ever know
the kind of person I really am,
I don't want to dress up myself in sham.
I want to go out with my head erect
I want to deserve all men's respect;
but here in the struggle for fame and wealth
I want to be able to like myself.
I don't want to look at myself and know that
I am bluster and bluff and empty show.
I never can hide myself from me;
I see what others may never see;
I know what others may never know,
I never can fool myself and so,
whatever happens I want to be
self-respecting and conscience free. (Edgar A. Guest)

Masks will not only cover what is hidden but they will also obscure your vision and dull your sensitivity to others. May God bless the truth of His Word into your life as you begin the continuous process of mask removal.

> "And be not conformed to this world: but be ye transformed by the renewing of your mind, that ye may prove what is that good, and acceptable, and perfect, will of God."[11]

Each day is a fresh start for you to move forward, revealing the Jesus in you.

Notes

5. Wikipedians. "The History of Masks," Wikipedia: The Free Encyclopedia, Wikimedia Foundation, last edited 2021.
6. Parfieneuk, I. and Stawinski, S. J. *Glosbe English-Latin Dictionary,* Poland, World Wide Web, 2011.
7. Sparks, Susan. "The Masks That We Wear," *Psychology Today*, New York City, James Thomas, October 20, 2015.
8. Dunbar, Paul Laurence. "We Wear the Mask," *The Complete Poems of Paul Laurence Dunbar,* New York, Dodd, Mead and Company, 1896, public domain.
9. Matthew. The Holy Bible (KJV), Matthew 7:3–4, Nashville, TN, Broadman and Holman, 1996.
10. Guest, Edgar A. *Myself,* Detroit, MI, Detroit Free Press, 1998, public domain.
11. Apostle Paul. The Holy Bible (KJV), Romans 12:2–3, Nashville, TN. Broadman and Holman, 1996.

Surviving Sexual Abuse

"Who shall separate us from the love of Christ? Shall tribulation, or distress, or persecution, or famine, or nakedness, or peril, or sword? As it is written, for thy sake we are killed all the day long; we are accounted as sheep for the slaughter. Nay, in all these things we are more than conquerors through him that loved us."
—Romans 8:35–37 (KJV)

In my teen years, it was unimaginable to openly talk about sex or sexual abuse. This was especially relevant to the abuse of children. These things were placed way back in the closet and whispered about among the adults. In my opinion, there was probably a very limited amount of statistics at that time because this sort of act was not often reported. However, today, known sexual abuse, by law in many states, must be reported by physicians, educators, social workers, clergy members, and family members who are made aware of such instances. Many of these actions still go unreported by the victim or their families. The evil act is a hidden part of family history.

Statistics show that one in four girls and one in six boys are sexually molested before the age of eighteen. Twenty-six percent of the victims of sexual abuse were between twelve and fourteen years of age, and 34 percent were younger than nine. Nearly 70 percent of all reports of sexual abuse (including adults) occur to children aged seventeen and under. Sexual abuse was thought to impact mostly female victims. More recently, we are learning new details about male victims since they are now speaking up and out at higher rates. Research regarding males (boys and men) in homeless shelters shows evidence of 50 percent or more sexual abuse occurrences.[12]

Today, experts agree that the incidence of sexual abuse is far greater than what is reported to authorities. The facts of sexual abuse remain somewhat cloudy since a large number of its victims suffer in silence. Most often, this abuse is perpetrated by an adult, male or female, who has access to the child by authority or kinship. Most offenders are known and trusted by their victim and their family; they may even be a family member. Research was done by Dr. Gene Abel asking voluntary sex offenders how many total offenses they had committed. The results were outrageous. Two hundred thirty-two child molesters reported 55,000 attempts, including 38,000 cases with a total of 17,000 victims. The average number of female victims was twenty, and the average number of male victims was fifteen. The chance of being caught, computed by Dr. Abel, was 3 percent.[13] It's sad to say, but sex predators can be anybody, including family members, good friends, clergy members, doctors, lawyers, or Indian chiefs.

The world of sexually abused children is forever changed. The trauma will always be a part of their consciousness. There are scars that may never be seen. The invisible scars are deep, painful, and yet bleeding. These children become adults who suffer in silence because of unhealed scars. Child abuse will cast shadows over a lifetime.

Not all survivors will experience the emotional impact of childhood sexual abuse (CSA). However, there are some emotions that are common among those who do. I have found guilt and shame to be the leaders. Some individuals, depending on their age, may feel they are to blame. Guilt, shame, and self-blame often lead to low self-esteem. Other emotional impacts include feeling dirty, depression, fear and anxiety, feelings of always having to please others due to low self-esteem, and flashbacks of the evil act.[14] Victims of CSA typically experience the act as a traumatic event. There are common reactions to this kind of trauma or shock, but at the same time, each person responds in their own unique way.

People react to the trauma of CSA on three different levels: physical, mental, and behavioral. These three levels may or may not occur simultaneously and influence the interactions with others. For example, having flashbacks or dreams (mental reactions) about the event will often trigger a physical reaction, such as an increase in heart rate, muscle tension, headaches, or rapid breathing. These reactions may lead to behaviors that help to avoid the stimuli that trigger the mental reaction (i.e., insomnia). It is vital to remember that these feelings are never the fault of the survivor. Many times, the victims have had their experiences denied, trivialized, distorted, or forgotten by family members and others who may know of the evil act. There are too many silent sufferers. Not because the abused didn't reach out; they tried but found no one who cared.[15] Delayed reporting of sexual abuse is a common reaction from someone who has experienced such a traumatic event. Reasons could be that the stigma associated with the abuse is embarrassing and possible retaliation from the offender. For many male victims, shame and secrecy are compounded by the fear that their own sexuality may be questioned, at least by others. We must look at the stories of children with the eyes of children, recognizing that a ten-year-old may have little language, knowledge, or a twisted understanding of human sexuality.[16]

"Brethren, I count not myself to have apprehended: but this one thing I do, forgetting those things which are behind, and reaching forth unto those things which are before." (Philippians 3:13 KJV)

I am a survivor, and this is (in part) my story. At the tender age of ten, I was sexually molested by a family member. I immediately told my mother, but nothing, I thought, was done. It was not until weeks later that I found out that the beating she had sustained by my offender was because she threatened to tell. Mom was often physically abused. The beatings, being a part of Mom's life, were not a surprise to my two sisters and (at that time) my two brothers. Months later, after my baby brother was born, my abuser entered my bedroom and proceeded to molest me again. I fought him the best I could using the tactics Mom's cousin had instructed me to use. Apparently, Mom had confided in her cousin about the first incident. Our cousin took me aside one day and instructed me what to do the next time this should occur, including how to get the upper hand of my abuser. Grab and pull for my life were the tactics she taught me to use, and I really got the upper hand. After I got away, leaving him in much pain, I took my prized possessions, my brand-new ice skates, and ran out into the cold, down the snow-covered road, to my grandma's house. Arriving at the house, in my pajamas, barefoot and in tears, I told Grandma all the ugly details. Grandpa had to restrain Grandma. She went and got the gun and started out of the house. She was madder than I had ever seen her. She finally simmered down and went to the evil one's house. After having some choice words and giving my perpetrator promises of great bodily harm, she packed my clothes and moved me out. The following years I lived with my two grandmothers. They only lived a few blocks from each other so it was easy for me to go from house to house. It seemed these two women had made a pact between them, from my birth, to ensure my care and needs were met. They did not neglect my sister and brothers. They also saw to their needs since the evil one did not always provide for them or Mom. We were all at his mercy. My grandmothers kept a watchful eye on them, always looking for evidence of physical or sexual abuse.

Two or three days after the tragic event, my grandmothers sat me down and began to talk to me regarding what had happened. They prayed and talked, talked and prayed, telling me that none of this was my fault and explaining the evils of this world we live in. They laid hands on me, and yes, they oiled me down. There were three things they told me to never forget.

1. I'm not to let what happened define who I am. I can be who I choose to be, who God has planned for me to be.
2. Don't judge myself because of what an evil person did to me.
3. This incident was just a weed in my garden of life. God is the keeper of my garden and He will always keep me. They said, "Weeds don't stop what God has planted and God is bigger than any weed. God is in the midst of my garden of life and He will never leave me."

After a while, I was allowed to visit my mom and sisters and brothers on the weekends. My abuser was always around, making snide and hateful remarks, but he never laid his hands on me again. I remember my grandmother's words and vowed I wasn't going to let him get the best of me; I was going to be somebody.

As time went by, memories of the incident faded and took a back seat in my mind.

This evil thing that happened to me did not stop my growth. I graduated high school, went to Dental Assisting School, got married, and had two beautiful children. I proceeded to get my bachelor's and master's degrees while raising a family, being a wife, working, and being the family caregiver. Somewhere down the line, I developed a type E personally: everything to everybody. I became busy trying to please everybody, especially my mother, and why? There was this little girl in me who was silently suffering, thinking she was not good enough, so she would please everybody by doing everything for everybody. Somewhere along life's journey, I had pushed the molestation way back in my mind, but I had also forgotten the teachings of my grandmothers. I was getting weary, and my marriage had gone sour. There was something wrong. I had accepted my call to the ministry, but I felt there was something else pulling at me. There was something that I needed to do.

After a bitter divorce, my friend asked me to enroll in a Biblical Counseling class. The first class, BC-1 Self Confrontation, was structured to teach you how to examine yourself biblically so you can live in a manner that was pleasing to God and help others do the same. The students in the class were from all walks of life, including spiritual leaders and laypeople. One of the requirements of the class was to prepare a self-confrontation testimony addressing one of your deep-seated issues according to God's Word. The instructor would periodically inquire as to our progress with our testimonies. Students would share the ideas they planned to use as the focus of their issues. Boy, did they have some stuff to confront. I didn't have anything as serious as theirs. They had some real problems. My minor concern of losing weight was nothing in comparison to some of the major challenges they had to face. This Bible-toting preacher lady didn't have any real significant problems. Little did I know or realize that my weight issue was a *real* weight issue. I, for real, needed to do the

Hebrews 12:1 "lay aside every weight." By the time the Holy Spirit guided me to my self-confrontation testimony, I had cried and prayed, prayed and cried. I began to diet and lose the heavy load of weight I carried for years, burdens that I carried and suffered in silence. I had to unload my heavy burden.

There were many tears as I began to peel back the layers of my heavy onion trying to reach the root of my problems. Since I was the most senior student in the class, my testimony had to have a title reflecting its author. I presented to my class the following on December 3, 1998:

THE OLD WOMAN'S PROBLEM[17]

I first thought my problem was simple, just a minor thing. A minor condition of being overweight was because of the inability to control or correct my eating habits. No big thing. Yeah, right! The more I began to investigate this area of my life, the more a little three-letter word popped up. It starts with *w,* has *h* in the middle, and ends with the letter *y*. You got it. That little big word is why.

- Why are you overweight?
- Why do you eat so much and so much of the wrong foods?
- Why must you snack?
- Why can't you control your cravings?

My answer was frustration. And of course, that little three-letter word popped up over and over again. To avoid speculation and get right down to the nitty-gritty, I changed the whys to whats. What is going on or what has gone on in my life that causes this habit of overeating?

My "old woman problem" that started with simply being overweight went from frustration to anger, back to frustration, on to wanting to please—always having to prove myself and not being able to say no only because I felt I had to please folks.

This escalated into a diagnostic procedure. This called for a biopsy. You know, take the little whys out for microscopic examination and convert them into whats. As the whys and whats began to surface, that all pointed to an old wound that I thought had healed. Exploratory surgery uncovered an old injury disguised as a scab that gave the appearance of being healed. Below the scab festered frustration, anger, and yes, low self-esteem. You see, I just had to please. I developed what is known in psychology circles as type E personality: "everything for everybody."

The Diagnosis

Making a long story short, let me just say that I have a history of sexual molestation and abuse. I thought I had adjusted well by putting it all behind me. The outer appearance looked good. After all, I considered myself to be a successful, attractive, educated, born-again, spirit-filled, joint heir with Jesus Christ and a child of Almighty God, but down deep inside, I had this insatiable desire to please everybody and prove myself to be the best in the sight of others. Why? What was the cause? Was it because the filthy stain of my molestation left its residue on me and I felt tainted by my past? Do I have feelings of worthlessness or am I afraid of being rejected? The biopsy showed I had all of the above.

However, this was not all bad. Some positive things came from wanting to be the best, wanting to please. It motivated me to do what negative-minded folks said I could not do (i.e., graduate high school, go to college, and get married). But I would have a house full of illegitimate kids. I proved them all wrong. But still, on the other hand, this need was frustrating because there were some folks I could never please no matter what I accomplished (i.e., my mother). Therefore, I could not say no due to my wanting-to-please infection. I was always tired, angry, and frustrated. This presented a domino effect. Everything played and fell on everything else. My work, family, spiritual growth, and relationship with God were compromised. So to please myself, I'd eat.

Before starting this class, I was on the way to realizing my issues. By teaching Sunday school, preparing workshops, and sermons, the messages and lessons always seemed to be for me. Yet I had the tendency to cover up, turn off the light, put on my ancestral fig leaf, and hide.

Are you aware that God and His Holy Spirit have a sense of humor? God has a way of bringing everything right down front, getting right in your face. What did He do? He set me up. He led me, by way of my friend, to this class titled "BC-1, Self-Confrontation." A class where God's Word was brought forth, peeling away the onion layers of my issues down to its core and pulling off the scab that covered my wound. The light in this class dispelled the darkness, I was disrobed, and my masks came off. This class prompted me to get up close in God's mirror. I saw the real me. My Lord, what a mess!

My Rx (Prescription) and Tx (Treatment Plan)

I can't begin to tell you all that this class has done for me, including the interaction with my classmates and teachers, the tears, and the prayers. But most of all, God's Word has truly blessed me. The following scriptures (paraphrased) have served as my Rx:

- Wanting to please: 1 Corinthians 10:31 ("Do all things to the Glory of God.")
  Ephesians 6:6–7 ("Strive to please God, not man or self.")
- Self-esteem: Psalm 139:14 ("I am fearfully and wonderfully made.")
  Genesis 1:27 ("I am made in my Holy Father's image.")
  John 3:16 ("God loved little old me so much that he sent His Son to save me from the penalty of sin.")
  1 John 4:4 ("The God in me is greater than he that is in this world.")

- When unsure: Philippians 4:14 ("With Christ I can do all things, He will give me the strength I need.")
- When anxious/afraid: Romans 8:28 ("God works all things for my good. I love Him and I have been called according to His purpose.") –

    1 Peter 5:7 ("I can cast all my worries upon God for He cares for me.") -
    2 Corinthians 12:9 ("God's grace is sufficient for me.")
- When angry: James 1:19-20 ("Be slow to anger.")

    Ephesians 4:26-27 ("Do not sin, don't let the sun go down on anger, don't give Satan opportunities.")
- My hope: Psalm 23 (God alone is my source, Only God, Always God, Totally God.)

My prescriptions are refillable and my treatment plan is continuous. As I continue to study God's Word and His Holy Spirit convicts me, I must continue the examination process. I will continue to ask, "Am I measuring up to God's Word and His plan for my life? God's Word is not to be used to increase just knowledge of Him but to change my life."

THE RESERVED OR (OPERATING ROOM)

The surgery is not over; there's more to come. The "old woman" with all her "old stuff" must be excised (cut upon to cut out) until this child of God is made perfect. As new whys and whats surface and begin their chamber of echoes in my life, surgery will be imminent. Through prayer, diligent study of God's Word, and by the power of the Holy Spirit, I will undergo more surgery and recover victorious.

I will not allow what happened define who I am. I will be who I choose to be, who God has planned for me to be. I won't judge myself because of what an evil person did to me. Weeds don't stop what God has planted, and God is bigger than any weed. God is in the midst of my garden of life, and He will never leave me.

> "Not as though I had already attained, either were already perfect: but I follow after, if that I may apprehend that for which also I am apprehended of Christ Jesus." -Philippians 3:12 (KJV)

Conclusion

If you drive while continually looking behind or in the rearview mirror, you will put yourself and any passengers in your car at risk. Your focus will be distracted and your vision limited.

Many have looked back on their lives, on past events—the good, bad and the ugly. Sir Winston Churchill reminded us that when we open past and present quarrels, we tend to misplace the future. In other words, if we are always lingering in the past, looking back at the past, there is little or no hope for the future. Looking back can freeze us in our yesterdays and keep us from successfully reaching our tomorrows.

When focusing on the past, the tendency is to pick the past apart and beat upon ourselves with *should've, could've, would've*. We are good at beating ourselves up with past sins, failures, and tragic events. Living in the past makes us prisoners and wastes the present time. Hanging on to the past does not allow for the healing of old hurts and painful memories. As a child of God, you can't be useful to ministry today by holding on to yesterday's mess-ups.

Instead of looking back, remember back. When you remember back, you see changes. You see how far you've come by the grace of our good Lord. When you remember back, you are able to see how the Lord has brought you out of the miry clay and put you on the rock to stay. Remember back and see what hardships you've endured, even childhood sexual abuse.

We can't live in the past and be fully alive. Don't let your yesterday's mess up your today. This will ruin your tomorrows. We must not look back on the painful memories of abuse or those experiences in life that haunt us. Leaving behind bad memories is necessary to experience what lies ahead. No, we can't always turn off the reruns of painful memories. But God will help us do what we can't do ourselves. God can bring healing to our painful memories as we confess our helplessness. God will deliver us from ourselves and help us say goodbye to yesterday, leaving the past behind where it should be. Remember back to the new creation that we are in Christ Jesus. Old things have passed away. Behold all things have become new.

> "Who shall separate us from the love of Christ? Shall tribulation, or distress, or persecution, or famine, or nakedness, or peril, or sword? As it is written, for thy sake we are killed all the day long; we are accounted as sheep for the slaughter. Nay, in all these things we are more than conquerors through him that loved us. For I am persuaded, that neither death, nor life, nor angels, nor principalities, nor powers, nor things present, nor things to come, nor height, nor depth, nor any other creature, shall be able to separate us from the love of God, which is in Christ Jesus our Lord." -Romans 8:35–39 (KJV)

> "The Lord bless thee, and keep thee: The Lord make His face shine upon thee, and be gracious unto thee: The Lord lift up His countenance upon thee, and give thee peace." -Numbers 6:24–26 (KJV)

Each day is a fresh start for you to move forward in the service of the Lord.

Instead of looking back; Remember back

NOTES

12. Langberg, Diane. "Shattered Innocence: Childhood Sexual Abuse," Forest, VA, *Christian Counseling Today,* vol. 23, no. 1, 2015.
13. Abel, Gene. *Abel Assessment of Sexual Interest,* Atlanta, GA, https://www.childmolestationprevention.org/pdfs/study.pdf, 1980.
14. Hall, M. and Hall, J. *The Long-Term Effects of Childhood Sexual Abuse,* Alexandria, VA, American Counseling Association, 2017.
15. Loyola Education Department. *Common Reactions to Sexual Assault,* Baltimore, MD, Loyola University Counseling Center, 2021.
16. Akulikowski. *Common Victim Behaviors of Survivors of Sexual Abuse,* PA, Pennsylvania Coalition Against Rape (PCARP), 2013.
17. Jefferson, LaRuth. *The Old Woman's Problem,* Southfield, MI, Biblical Counseling, Self-Confrontation (BC-1), 1998.

Section 2
Forgiveness and Love

Forgive Like Jesus Did (LJD)

"Put on therefore, as the elect of God, holy and beloved, bowels of mercies, kindness, humbleness of mind, meekness, longsuffering; Forbearing one another, and forgiving one another, if any man have a quarrel against any: even as Christ forgave you, so also do ye."
—Colossians 3:12–13 (KJV)

Sunday after Sunday, many churchgoers pray Matthew 6:12. "Forgive us our debts, as we also have forgiven our debtors." Or maybe they use the passage from Luke 11:4 (NIV). "Forgive us our sins, for we also forgive everyone who sins against us." We pray this prayer or we sing this prayer with all its beautiful chord changes and harmony. As we do this, we rarely give a thought or even ponder if we have really, fully forgiven all those who have offended us. God commands us to forgive. We are to forgive *like Jesus did* (LJD).

After a young man shot five young girls to death in West Nickels, Pennsylvania, there was a single-word headline in the news. The one-word headline was "Forgiveness."[18] This one-word headline got media attention worldwide. All of us need to understand and come to terms with the issues of forgiveness.

Forgiveness is a word we both hate and love. This grace of forgiveness, LJD for us, is welcomed by all God's chosen people. When Jesus died for our sins, He was the blood atonement for our forgiveness, thereby releasing us from our sin debt. It's all because of Christ that our sins are forgiven.

God presses the delete button on His heavenly computer. He doesn't send our sins to a temporary recycling bin just in case He needs to remind us of them. He totally removes them from the hard drive. That's why we love the word *forgiveness*. However, when it comes to us forgiving others, this forgiveness becomes a problem. We recycle the hurt and the offense over and over again and look for ways to get revenge.

Remember our friend in Matthew 18, the parable of the wicked unforgiving servant? He was forgiven a gigantic debt by his master but refused to forgive his fellow servant a small debt. Yes, I did call this unforgiving servant our friend. If we are honest with Mr. or Ms. Self, we know we are somewhere in the boat of unforgiveness. We may not be in the bow (front) steering the boat, hanging out at the stern (back), on the starboard (right) side, or on the port (left side), but we are somewhere on board.

Colossians 3:12 addresses God's chosen, the elect, the beloved of God. These are the ones who are to forgive. These were words that originally belonged to the Jews. The apostle Paul, by the unction of the Holy Spirit, gives them to us since God's love and grace flow to the ends of the earth, and by the shed blood of Jesus Christ, we were adopted into the family of God.[19] So as children of God, the elect, we are to clothe ourselves in compassion, kindness, humility, gentleness, and patience. We are to bear with each other and forgive whatever grievances we may have against one another. Forgive as the Lord forgave you. Forgive LJD. We are not to act or respond as the world does when someone offends or mistreats us. We are not to be mean-spirited, impatient, hold a grudge, or seek revenge. We are commanded to forgive.

Now understand when we forgive, we aren't excusing what was done or sanctioning immorality or evil deeds. Forgiving is not the avoidance of conflict. There are a lot of us who do not like conflict so we often skirt around issues like a square dance. We keep silent as hurt feelings turn into grudge holding, bitterness, resentment, anger, retaliation, and vindictiveness. All this because we fail to release and forgive.

Forgiveness is difficult because it cost so much. When we forgive, we accept the loss or hurt without demanding any reimbursement, revenge, or satisfaction of any kind. Forgiveness means we suffer so that the offending party can be restored to fellowship with us. When we practice forgiveness, we hold no grudges and nurse no resentment. This means we yield a claim that might be rightfully ours and release the offender from a justified penalty LJD.

Forgiving is hard; it's not easy. It's much more than saying or singing a memorized prayer. We struggle with forgiveness because it's contrary to our human nature. Our natural tendency is to get even, to lay our religion down and lay hands on the perpetrator. It's much easier to brood, hold a grudge, make people sweat than to implement mercy and release the offender. God wants His children, His elect, to exhibit His qualities, to show His love, His grace and mercy, and His willingness to forgive.

God's plan was the core of Jesus' ministry. Jesus set the protocol for forgiving when He said in Matthew 18:15–18 (paraphrased), "If you have something against someone, first go to them. Then after that, you may need to draw others into the process of confrontation and reconciliation." How often do we go to everybody but the offender with whom we have the issue? They may not know that they have offended you or that there is a problem. We hold on to stuff allowing it to metastasize like a cancer. This affects us by eating our life away, making those around us miserable, disconnecting ourselves from God and giving place to Satan to send us down a spiral of other sins.

The practice of forgiveness is a ministry that sets an example to the world by showing that there is a better way than retaliation. There will be offenses in this life. We are going to be insulted, betrayed, persecuted, mistreated, and abused. Not one of us can escape the shock of offenses. Those who have not experienced the indignation and hot flashes of anger are dead. Jesus said in John 16:33 that we would have trouble, tribulation, and offenses. God made us an emotional people. It's all right to be angry and hurt, but it's not all right to let that hurt and anger turn into hate and bitterness. We must root up the thorns of bitterness so that the rose of forgiveness can bloom and flourish.

I know there are many questions about this forgiveness thing. In Matthew 18:21–22 (KJV), Peter said, "How oft shall my brother sin against me, and I forgive him? Till seven times?" Don't forget the age-old statement regarding forgiving and not forgetting. You may have more, but let's examine the first one. Jesus told Peter, "Not seven times, but seventy times seven." He did not mean to forgive 490 times. Jesus took this to show that forgiveness is endless and continuous. In other words, you can't put a limit on forgiveness. How many times has Jesus forgiven you for the same old sin plus all your new ones? What if Jesus stopped the fifth time around? Wouldn't you be in a mess?

Let's examine "the forgive but can't forget problem." Someone said, "To say you'll forgive but can't forget is like burying the hatchet with the handle sticking out."[20] Forgetting an offense is impossible for us. Whenever we honestly try to extend forgiveness and think the issue is over, it somehow has a way of replaying in our memory bank, even months or years later. Only God forgives, forgets, and wipes our slate clean. However, He is God. Not forgetting doesn't mean you haven't forgiven someone because you have a flashback about the situation. You remember what happened, but there's no more pain, no bitterness or anger. It's like a sore that has healed and leaves a scar. The scar is there, but it no longer hurts. When old memories surface, it means you have to reaffirm, shore up your commitment to forgive, release it, and move on. When you are able to forgive and release, this reflects the real work of grace in your life.

We must release and let go of old hurts and offenses for if we refuse, guess what. No, don't guess. Let me tell you what happens. There is a codicil, an addendum, a postscript to the prayer we pray on Sundays. Matthew 6:14–15 (KJV) reads, "For if ye forgive men their trespasses, your heavenly Father will also forgive you: But if ye forgive not men their trespasses, neither will your Father forgive your trespasses." If this is not clear to you, let me unpack it for you. When we pray, "Forgive us our debts, as we also have forgiven our debtors," what we are really praying is "Lord, if I refuse to forgive them, please don't forgive me. Lord, if I hold a grudge against them, please hold a grudge against me." Why would Jesus attach this codicil? Because without it, we would fall into sin of disobedience and would be denying our common ground as sinners in need of God's forgiveness.

This codicil "For if you forgive other people when they sin against you, your heavenly Father will also forgive you. But if you do not forgive others their sins, your Father will not forgive your sins" may seem to make God's forgiveness dependent on our forgiving. God does not forgive us because we forgive others but out of His unending mercy. God does not require any works or payment for His mercy, but He does require us to show mercy to others, LJD. Having received forgiveness, we are commanded to pass it forward. So you ask, "Who me? Forgive them?" Yes you, my Christian brothers and sisters. This is not optional. God commanded it, Jesus did it, and we too must do it!

Theologian C. S. Lewis noted that the act of forgiveness is remarkable until we have to do the forgiving.[21] Forgiveness is one of the greatest challenges to human nature and is harder than any preacher makes it out to be. Some of us love to hang on to old stuff. I spoke to a Christian friend who for years has carried unforgiveness toward someone who hurt her daughter. The person is now deceased, yet she continues to hold on to all the pain and hurt they caused. As she carries this burden, her relationship with Christ has suffered, her prayers are weak, and she is troubled as the turmoil mounts within her. I've heard her make statements like "I can't forgive him. You don't know how he treated my child. I have good reasons not to forgive. I just can't do it. He ought to pay." She is most miserable. She is in a self-made prison, a sea of unforgiveness. She has let the past paralyze her. She wants to get even, but the offender is dead. She is stuck in the past, tied to the evil of another that robs her of the future God has planned for her. I don't say this out of criticism or judgment but out of my own experience. Been there, done that. I know forgiveness is hard. I also know that failure to practice forgiving and to seek revenge is not the way of Christ. God has said vengeance is His; He will repay. We are not to repay evil for evil. We must let go of the thoughts and fantasies of revenge. We must look to the future rather than the past.

Forgiveness is like many other principles of the Bible. It takes love and the power of the Holy Spirit working within you to manifest. Think of it this way. You wouldn't be saved without God's intervention. You can't be healed without His power. You can't express or exercise the "Fruit of the Spirit" without the power of the Holy Spirit. Just as you can't be saved, be healed, or manifest the "Fruit of the Spirit" without

God's power, you can't forgive without it. It takes the Holy Spirit working within you to help you forgive. Without God, Jesus, and the Holy Spirit, we can do nothing.

So how do we begin to forgive? There is no easy road to forgiveness. Don't let anyone tell you, "Just do it. Let it go." Simplistic, trite answers only demean those who suffer and pick at their wound. Forgiving another takes work, time, and much prayer. It's something we must practice and affirm every day; otherwise, our Christian profession of faith is in vain and we make a mockery of the precious blood of Jesus. It begins with thanksgiving and recognition that we have been forgiven by God.

Remember the cost of God's forgiveness to us? His Son was born to die for our sins. Even though we were not present at Calvary, our sinful hands helped to nail His hands to the cross. Water and blood were released from His body to wash us clean and cover our sins, and He responded, "Father forgive them for they know not what they do" (Luke 23:24). We are the beneficiaries of the crucified one. The cry of Jesus to forgive is a cry we are to echo in our own lives, in our families, our work place, our churches, and our day-to-day life. For most of us, this forgiveness thing is a process that we live and mature into with the help of the Holy Spirit. Sometimes the pain is too much, the wound too raw, the memories too real. On those days, all we can do is choose to want to forgive and pray, "Lord, please help me to forgive." We choose and want to forgive because this is the choice Christ made and we are striving to forgive LJD. Forgiving those who have wronged us is the salve that begins to heal our wounds. It may not change the one who hurt you, but your life will be more grace filled, alive, and Christlike.

Below is a poem a dear friend of mind, a Detroit poet, wrote for a forgiveness workshop that our church sponsored.

Forgive: Get in the Game[22]

> Forgiveness is something we all must do. It benefits both you and me. Whenever you are feeling blue, forgiveness is probably overdue.

Forgiveness is what God asks of you; to forgive your neighbor, forgive your spouse and forgive the ones that share your house. Forgive the ones that have hurt you, then after that, forgive you too!

Forgive the ones that caused you pain, for believe it or not, God loves them just the same. So, get over it is what to do. You can't change them, you can only change you.

So, as you can tell, without a doubt, forgiveness is what it's all about. If pleasing the Lord is your aim, then forgiving others is the name of the game. Get in the Game!

Forgive! Let the healing begin. There are stripes to heal your broken heart and mend your wounded spirit. Forgive! There's a tree that will sweeten the bitterness in your soul. Forgive! Lay down your burden, your heavy load. Get free! Don't let the chains of unforgiveness keep you bound. Remember to include yourself in the forgiveness process. Forgiving others includes you too. Why condemn yourself when 1 John 1:9 (KJV) tells us, "If we confess our sins, he is faithful and just to forgive us our sins, and to cleanse us from all unrighteousness"?

May the Holy Spirit help us to comprehend more fully the amazing forgiving grace that God applied to all our sins and wrongdoings. May He help us show that same forgiving grace to all those that have done us wrong, LJD.

EPILOGUE

If you have read "Surviving Sexual Abuse," you probably noticed that there was no mention of forgiveness. After my grandmothers got themselves together and the offense had some space, they began to talk to me about forgiving my abuser. They explained that this was what Jesus did and what God wanted all His children to do, including

His old children like them. Even though my grandmothers were very upset over the past event and because they loved the Lord and wanted to do the right thing, they forgave my offender. They took me over Matthew 6, the Model Prayer, and explained verses 14 and 15. I loved my grandmothers and I loved Jesus so I said that I would forgive that man too. They made me repeat this forgiveness every time I prayed or said grace at dinner. I would pray, "Jesus I forgive all those who have hurt me. Please help me to hold on to this forgiveness." As the years went by, there was very little contact with my abuser and the contact that we did have was never very pleasant. I made it through the following thirty-odd years on my knees and with my grandmother's support and prayers.

My offender became ill and was in a hospital some forty-five miles from his family. Since I taught at the college about five miles from the hospital and was also considered the family caregiver, I was asked to pay him a visit. I prayed as I traveled the five miles to the hospital, asking the Lord to give me strength and a kind loving spirit. When I entered his room and his eyes focused on me, he began to cry and said, "I never thought you would come to see me." We had a peaceful conversation. He began to tell me of his personal financial status. Because of our past relationship, this seemed weird to me. I wasn't sure what I was supposed to do with this information. I visited him two or three more times and he repeated his same financial status. Finally, he told me to make sure I gave this information to my siblings. You see, he had two sets of children. Shortly after my last visit, he was released.

Several weeks later, as I made my forty-five-mile drive from work in a snowstorm at night, I suddenly found myself parked in front of his house. I have no memory of how I got there, but I was parked in front of the house where my abuse had taken place. I had not been on that street or anywhere near that house in over thirty-five years. Here I was, in my snow-laden car, in front of my abuser's house.

I got out of my car, treaded through the knee-high snow, and knocked on the door. I was greeted with "What are you doing here, and what do you want?" I simply said, "I just came by to see how he is doing." I was allowed to go upstairs to his room. Old feelings started to mount up in me. I prayed, "Lord, please help me."

As I entered his room, focusing his eyes on me, he told my greeter to leave us alone. Again, he began to cry. I asked him, "What is wrong?" He explained that he wanted and needed me to forgive him for what he had done and the pain he caused me. I told him that I had forgiven him long ago and I forgive him still. He cried more and asked me to pray for him.

We discussed salvation and did the Romans 10:9 scripture. "That if you confess with your mouth, 'Jesus is Lord,' and believe in your heart that God raised him from the dead, you will be saved." I felt like a priest hearing a confession. Afterward, I prayed and he prayed. He then requested that I sing "Jesus Loves Me; This I Know for the Bible Tells Me So." He joined in on, "Yes, Jesus loves me."

After we finished singing, I kissed him on his forehead and departed. It was around 11:00 p.m. in February 1985. Around 4:00 that next morning, my abuser died. He died saved and forgiven.

Very often forgiveness is not just for us but for those who have been abused and mistreated. The offender must be given the opportunity to seek forgiveness from those they have mistreated and or abused. Forgiveness is for everyone, the abused as well as the abuser. We must always be ready and willing to forgive no matter what the circumstances. Ready to forgive just like Jesus did.

Rev. Martin Luther King Jr., known for his famous quotes and speeches, enlightened our minds when he stated in order to forgive, we must love unconditionally, remembering that forgiveness is an attitude and not just a pretentious act.[23]

> "Forbearing one another, and forgiving one another, if any man have a quarrel against any: even as Christ forgave you, so also do ye." -Colossians 3:13 (KJV)

Each day is a fresh start for you to forgive LJD.

Notes

18. Lawrenz, Mel. *How Forgiveness Works,* Brookfield, WI, http://www.preching.com, 2010.
19. Apostle Paul. The Holy Bible (KJV), Galatians 4:4–6, Nashville, TN, Broadman and Holman, 1996.
20. Unknown. *Our Daily Bread,* October 19, Grand Rapids, MI, Discovery House Publishers Ministries, 1999.
21. Lewis, C. S. *Mere Christianity,* p. 115, New York City, Touchstone Books, 1996.
22. May-Watson, Barbara A. "Forgiveness: Get in the Game," Southfield, MI, by permission, son Wayne Watson, 2021.
23. King Jr., Martin Luther. *The Meaning of Forgiveness,* Stanford, CA, Research and Education Institute (Stanford.edu), 1954.

I Wish Jesus Hadn't Said That

> "Ye have heard that it hath been said, Thou shalt
> love thy neighbour, and hate thine enemy.
> But I say unto you, Love your enemies, bless them that curse you,
> do good to them that hate you, and pray for them which despitefully
> use you, and persecute you; That ye may be the children of your
> Father which is in heaven: for he maketh his sun to rise on the evil
> and on the good, and sendeth rain on the just and on the unjust."
> —Matthew 5:43–45 (KJV)

I've got some good news and some bad news. The good news is that God is a God of love and grace. This means that God, out of His great love and grace, accepts us in spite of who we are and how we are. These are easy truths to come to, especially the "in spite of" part. When we understand that God accepts us "in spite of," it is good news. The word *gospel* means good news. Believing the good news that God's great love and grace accept us in spite of is the beginning of salvation. The good news is that God is a God of love and grace. But I also have some bad news. The bad news is that God is a God of love and grace. Confused? Let me explain.

Jonah heard this as bad news. You remember the story of Jonah. God called Jonah to go to Nineveh, the capital of the Assyrians, the hated, cruel enemy of the Israelites. But regardless of how "those people" treated God's chosen ones, regardless of the animosity between the two of them, God told Jonah to go into the enemy camp and preach of His "in spite of" love and grace. Jonah didn't want to go preach to "those people," his enemy and the enemy of Israel.

Jonah saw God's grace and love as good news and bad news. It was good news that God loved him and extended grace and mercy toward him "in spite of" how he was, but he didn't want to go and tell "those people" about his wonderful God. So for him, this was bad news. He didn't want his enemy to experience God's "in spite of" love and grace. It's the "in spite of" part that makes it difficult. To Jonah, those mean evil people didn't deserve God's grace or His love.

If we are honest with ourselves, we sometimes feel like Jonah. We know some people we feel don't deserve God's love let alone His grace. There are some people we don't want God to love or show grace. "In spite of" is too inclusive for us. There ought to be some people excluded out of the scope of God's love and grace. But God loves "in spite of." It would be easier to live with the bad news of God's "in spite of" love if it didn't involve us. God chooses to love all because He is God almighty.

In my spiritual selective Alzheimer's moments, I think we ought to have a choice of who we love or hate. But God's love involves us. Jesus, the Son of God, described our involvement in God's "in spite of" love this way: "You have heard that it was said, 'You shall love your neighbor and hate your enemy.' But I say to you, love your enemies …" I wish Jesus hadn't said that. In order to understand what this text says, you must first hear it as bad news.

Jesus said, "Love your enemies … bless those who curse you, do good to those who hate you, and pray for those who spitefully use you and persecute you …" I know you wish Jesus hadn't said that. Until you have that person in mind, you will not really understand this text. There are lots of areas where we can find enemies. It's easy. All we need are some strong differences. The meaning of *enemy* that quickly comes to mind is enemy nations, those who oppose our values or infringe on our interests. Our latest enemy is terrorism, which threatens our national and personal safety. But we can also find enemies here at home. We have political enemies and religious enemies—those who do not value what we value or believe what we believe. Maybe you have an enemy in your business, an evil competitor. Perhaps you have a rival for another's affections who has proven to be an enemy. Don't you have people who have wronged you or hurt you and maybe are still hurting you? The enemy is not necessarily some faraway, abstract person. It's the husband who had an affair while his wife was nursing their newborn. Jesus is saying to that wife, "Love him." It's the coworker who spread those untrue rumors that led to your unfair dismissal. Jesus says to the one who was dismissed, "Love your coworker." It's the investor who defrauded an elderly couple out of their retirement savings. Jesus says to the elderly couple, "Love that investor." It's the friend who told your secrets and confidences and ruined your reputation. Jesus says, "Love that friend." It's the muggers and thieves, the rapist and murderers. Jesus says, "Love them, bless them, do them good, and pray for them …"

Lord knows I wish Jesus hadn't said that. Loving your enemy is a real problem in our society today. When someone hurts or threatens us, we want to retaliate with words and/or actions. We want to get even. Now be honest with yourself, you don't want to love your enemies. You want to put your Bible down, take off your earrings, tuck your cross inside your shirt, and "lay hands" on them just a little bit. You want to anoint them up side their heads one or two times, talk about them, turn away from them if you see them coming your way, make them pay in some way or another. If you're not in a position to retaliate, you wait until something happens to them so you can gloat, saying, "God don't like ugly, and He's not particular about pretty," or "They only got what they deserved." We don't stop to consider how ugly we look to God.

Without the blood of Jesus covering us, or how God, through His "in spite of" love and grace, does not give us what we deserve, we look really messy. Jesus said, "Love 'them people' that mess with you, bless 'them people' that curse, do good to your haters, pray for them who spitefully use you and persecute you and why? "That you may be sons of your Father in heaven. He gives His sunlight to both the evil and the good, and sends rain on the just and on the unjust too."

You say, "Your enemies don't deserve your love". Jesus said, "Love them." In loving them, you will be acting as true children of your

Father in heaven. This calls for us, God's children, to reflect the image of God our Father. God has made us in His image (Genesis 1:26–27) and called us to display godlikeness in the way we relate to our enemies, for God is love (1 John 4:8, 16). When we treat both our friends *and* enemies with love, grace, and kindness, we are behaving like our heavenly Father, who is no respecter of persons. He bestows His blessings of sunshine and rain on all sinners—those recovering sinners and those not yet recovered. Jesus is calling us to a higher standard of behavior than that of this world.

Here are a few words that give us the picture of love. We often read them in the context of loving the people who we want to love. Think about how these words apply to your enemies. Pick one or two of your enemies. Now don't sit there pretending that you don't have somebody you can't stand. You must have at least one. Think about that person or persons who have done you wrong and see how Jesus would have you treat them.

> "Love suffers long and is kind; love does not envy; love does not parade itself, is not puffed up; love does not behave rudely; does not seek its own; is not provoked; thinks no evil; love does not rejoice in iniquity, but rejoices in the truth; love bears all things, believes all things, hopes all things, endures all things. Love never fails."[24]

I wish the spirit of God had not inspired Paul to write that. John 3:16 says, God so loved everybody in the world, the good, the bad, and the ugly. First John 2:2 tells us that Jesus died for the sins of the whole world, even those who hate Him, even those who do not believe in Him. As Rev. Dr. Martin Luther King Jr. came to the end of his sermon, he fed the congregation's soul with powerful words by simply stating that the death and cross of Jesus Christ allowed the world to see the love of our God that has permeated the history of humankind.[25] We know what love looks like in a world filled with hatred, distrust, bitterness, pain, mistreatment, and abuse. Isaac

Watts penned in the second verse of his hymn "When I Survey the Wondrous Cross," "See, from His head, His hands, His feet, sorrow, and love flow mingled down. Did ever such love and sorrow meet or thorns composed so rich a crown." The message from God is that love is the only way. It's the only way to live on the earth. If we believe in Jesus at all, we must say to our enemies, "I love you, and you can't do a thing about it."

With Jesus walking with us, we will find the strength to love our enemies, to bless those who curse us, and to pray for those who despitefully use us. Don't seek revenge; instead, seek to bless your enemies. If you can let go of your anger long enough to pray for them, you will discover a wonderful benefit for you won't have time to hate or be bitter. When you pray the "in spite of" kind of love and grace for your enemies, you put yourself in a position to receive love and grace in return. Loving your enemy is the biblical alternative to revenge.

Here are five things that will help you love your enemies:

- Don't live in your hurts. Banking those hurts will make it harder to forgive. Peter was living in his hurts when he said in Matthew 18:21, "Lord, how often shall my brother sin against me and I forgive him, up to seven times?" Forgive like Jesus did for us. His forgiveness and love are limitless. We must deal with each hurt with love, grace, and forgiveness.
- Do not reply in anger. Proverbs 15:1 reminds us, "A gentle answer turns away wrath, but a harsh word stirs up anger." Reflect your Father's image and surprise your enemy with kind words.
- Be patient with annoying people. Like mosquitoes, some people persistently annoy us. Patience is a virtue.
- Pray for those who hurt you. Jesus did so Himself when He prayed for those who crucified Him (Luke 23:24). You will find it very hard to hate someone for whom you are praying.
- Surprise the next person who hurts you. Take the Jesus alternative to getting even and replace the spirit of retaliation with Christlikeness "in spite of" love.

We must practice this "in spite of love." We must pray for a little more Jesus in our lives. I'm really glad about what Jesus said of God and Himself, "For God so loved the world that He gave His one and only Son, that whoever believes in Him shall not perish but have eternal life." We are the "whoevers" that God so loved and Jesus gave His life for. We are the "them people" who were once enemies of Christ. But "in spite of," He loved us and loves us still. Jesus loved his enemies, and we must do the same. Love others as God has loved us and like Jesus did. Loving others, even our enemies, should be the natural mindset for all God's children. Pray for more "in spite of" love and grace.

Conclusion

Remember back in the day when we pulled petals off a flower while saying, "Love me? Love me not?" We did this seeking to know if the one we had a crush on cared for us. Today we say, "I might like them, but I *don't* love them." To love or not to love, that is the question. My friends, if you profess Jesus Christ as your Lord and Savior, you don't have this option. To love is a "must do." God's children are to be known by their love for others. It has been said that God has established a very clear birthmark by which His children, who have been birthed by the Holy Spirit, ought to be known. Love is the birthmark of the Christian. Without the birthmark of love, other people really won't know who you are.[26]

Love is in demand because this world is full of hate, violence, vengeance, envy, strife, bigotry, evil, and self-centeredness. Tina Turner's song "What's Love Got to Do with it?" asks a good question for the body of Christ. The answer can be summed up in one word: everything!

It is imperative that we learn to love like God loves. It is the highest characteristic of God our Father. It is the one attribute in which all others blend in harmony. The love of God underlines all that He has done, all that He is doing, and all that He will ever do. God's love is unconditional and undeserved. It is love with feet, meaning love with action. Like our heavenly Father, we must show love, not only with words but also through our actions.

God's love showed up as a little bitty baby born to die for the sins of this world. God's love showed up at the cross of Calvary, where Jesus hung, bled, and died for our sins, past, present, and future. "Greater love has no one than this, than to lay down one's life for his friends" (John 15:13). Jesus was sent by God as His supreme gift to you and me that we may have hope, peace, joy, and love.

I realize there are some folks who are hard to love. It's not easy. But God said, "Love them," like He loves us. Living in love reveals a genuine Christian lifestyle. Are you living in love or seething in bitterness, hate, unforgiveness, and retaliation? Let me ask you this: how easy is it for someone to love you even with your bad attitude and even in your mess? Jesus loves you, in spite of your bad attitude and all your mess. Without God's love, grace, mercy, and guidance, we would be a real mess waiting to happen.

Love is basic to our walk with our Lord. Failure to love disqualifies all we may say or do. Our vertical relationship with God is measured by our horizontal relationship with others. Our love for God is measured by our love for others.

WWJD? What would Jesus do? No! It should be WDJD? What did Jesus do? Love! What's love got to do with it? *Everything!*

> "And thou shalt love the Lord thy God with all thy heart, and with all thy soul, and with all thy mind, and with all thy strength: this is the first commandment. And the second is like, namely this, Thou shalt love thy neighbour as thyself. There is none other commandment greater than these." Mark 12:30–31 (KJV)

Each day is a fresh start for you to love like Jesus loves.

Notes

24. Apostle Paul. "On Love," 1 Corinthians 13:4–8 (KJV), Nashville, TN, Broadman and Holman, 1996.
25. King Jr., Martin Luther. *Loving Your Enemies.* Montgomery, AL, http://www.kinginstitute.stanford.edu/king-papers/, 1957.
26. Evans, Tony. *Book of Illustrations: Love,* p. 196, Chicago, IL, Moody Publishers, 2009.

Section 3
Inner Conflict

Chains That Bind

> "Such as sit in darkness and in the shadow of death, being bound in affliction and iron, He brought them out of darkness and the shadow of death, and brake their bands in sunder."
> —Psalm 107:10, 14 (KJV)

Have you ever watched a dog that is chained? Have you ever noticed how hard he tries to go a little farther but the chain always holds him in the same place, never letting him go? When people take their dogs on a walk, they leash them and sometimes use chains to keep the dog from going anywhere other than where the owner wants the dog to go. The dog really has no freedom outside of a three- to four-foot radius.

Unfortunately, in the church, many people are chained and bound. They remain in the same place rather than moving forward into what God wants to do in their lives. They remain in the same place where things are familiar, even if it is uncomfortable. Many are chained to their possessions, past failures, sexual sins, religious traditions, pride, and the list goes on. What holds you back? What frustrates you? Where do you always find a road block? Some are chained by wrong emotions and can't seem to find peace. There are habits and addictions that can't seem to be broken. You are in bondage when you are oppressed by anyone or anything and your focus can't expand to a wider territory.

Part of the spiritual warfare we all are engaged in is found in the desire of our enemy, Satan. He is the thief who comes to steal, kill, and destroy and to keep us in bondage and all chained up, preventing us from being of service to our Lord and Savior. Satan is a liar, and a deceiver, and the truth is not in him. My God is in the chain-busting business. When He sent His Son Jesus, all chains were loosed. The chains that can hold us are the ones we allow. Let's find the freedom Christ is offering you, the very freedom He died to give to you. We have to step out on faith and believe God has more for our lives than what we are experiencing.

In the New Testament, chains have already been broken. In John 8:30–38 (paraphrased), Jesus said to His disciples, "You are truly my disciples if you live as I tell you to, and you will know the truth, and the truth will set you free." Then some replied, "But we are descendants of Abraham and have never been slaves to any man on earth! What do you mean 'set free'?" Jesus responded, "You are slaves of sin, every one of you. And slaves don't have rights, but the Son has every right there is! So if the Son sets you free, you will be free indeed."

Then in Galatians 5:1, Paul tells us, "Stand fast therefore in the liberty wherewith Christ hath made us free, and be not entangled again with the yoke of bondage." Because of Christ Jesus, we are slaves no more but heirs. Rather than embracing the freedom we find in Christ Jesus, we often allow ourselves to remain chained to the past and the things of this world. As we see in scripture, we do not need to do that! We do not have to live that way. The chains are broken! We have been set free through the sacrifice of Jesus on the cross. We are now a part of God's family and are now heirs and not slaves. We are to be slaves of righteousness rather than slaves of sin. The apostle Paul points out in Romans 6:18 that we are set free from sin, that sin does not have to hold us in bondage anymore.

Let's take a look at the bondage and chains of biblical times that are still binding up Christians today and see how Jesus opened the door to freedom. If Christ could set people free way back then, He can set us free today. However, we must realize some followed Christ and were set free while others remained chained to the sins and unrighteousness to which they had grown accustomed, not realizing how fulfilling a walk with Christ could be.

There's the rich young ruler of Mark 10:17–27. This chain was one the young man chose, thereby remaining restricted for the rest of his life. Jesus told him how to break the chain, but he was too attached to all his stuff to walk away and experience a new life that would be worth more than any amount of money he could ever attain. Jesus told him to give up his possessions and follow Him. The rich young ruler was too chained to his material possessions and temporary stuff to see the eternal value of what Jesus was offering him. His money had become his idol and he did not recognize that Jesus wanted to be his Savior.

We all struggle with this at various points in our lives. Ask yourself these questions and be honest with yourself:

- Do you control your possessions, or do your possessions control you?
- Are you spending more time trying to acquire more, or do you spend your time looking to give to others?

Jesus told us how to break that chain. All we have to do is give up some stuff and follow Him. We must choose the eternal over the temporary.

What about the woman at the well in John 4:5–30? She was chained to sexual sin. She could not escape who she had been. The whole town knew who she was. One day, she met a man who knew everything she had ever done. Jesus exposed her sin and helped her to see what she was looking for was true love, love that could only be found in Him. Christ wanted her to experience a love that would change her life rather than keep her chained to sexual sin that would only leave her empty.

Sexual sin runs rampant and is an epidemic in our culture today. The entertainment industry thrives on sex and promotes it in nearly everything it produces. Advertising and marketing agencies have bought into the idea that "sex sells." Commercials and advertisements contain all kinds of sexual suggestions. As our culture becomes more sexually driven, we see a rise in chains of sexual immorality that destroys lives, homes, and families. Satan's type of love will never equal real true love. God, who is the very definition of love, stands against this immorality. This chain has already been broken. Through Jesus, we too can be set free from sexual sin just as the woman at the well was set free.

Peter in John 21:15–17, had denied Christ and had failed on other occasions. Peter was chained to the past, to the failures and mistakes he had made only days earlier. He could not see beyond that moment when the rooster crowed until Christ commissioned him to be more than his mistakes and failures. Christ would not allow Peter to remain chained to the past. Jesus broke the chain and set him free to be a leader of the church. Christ would not allow Peter to remain in that past mistake or be defined by his failures.

Are you chained to your past? Can you look back and see things that happened previously that may have you stuck? Break loose! You've been chained far too long. Forgiveness from God frees us to be a new man or woman in Him rather than living under the mistakes we made long ago. Christ died to set us free from those sins. He took each one of those failures to the cross. The sin debt has been paid and those chains have been broken. The shame of each sin Jesus bore on the cross.

In the Gospel of Luke 13:10–13, there was a woman who was bent over. As Jesus was teaching in the synagogue on the Sabbath, He saw a seriously handicapped woman who had been bent over for eighteen years and was unable to straighten herself. Jesus called to her; He touched her and broke the chain that had her bound and instantly she could stand straight and was healed. Sickness is a part of life that we would rather not experience. The beauty is that the day of miracles has not ended. He is still Jehovah Rapha and continues to heal individuals each day. The sickness we have does not have to define who we are. God can be glorified through it all as He works in our lives and helps us to overcome our infirmities. Be open to see the Great Physician at any time, and let Him go to work in your lives.

Nicodemus, in John 3:1–20, illustrates the church today. We say we are Christians. We may even act religiously daily and attend church as good Christians. The problem is that we are motivated and shackled by religion rather than being led by faith as God has called us to be. We changed only what we are doing instead of opening ourselves up to allow God to change who we are. Nicodemus, a Pharisee, was among the crowd that could never get beyond religion to experience true faith that comes from a walk with Jesus. The Pharisees stayed chained to the law and tradition. They held on to the law, but their motivation was twisted. They did it to be seen by others as being holy and to be revered as religious leaders. They missed out on what could have taken them to new heights. Nicodemus was not content with staying in the same place. He knew there had to be more. He went to see if Christ could break the chains religion had placed on his heart. Jesus gave Nicodemus the way to change his life. Jesus called him to step out on faith and accept Him as Christ, his Savior. The chains of religion have been broken. There is life in the faith we have in Jesus Christ. We look to Him instead of remaining bound to religious traditions. Religion never changed anyone; it only changes what they do.

Faith in Christ always changes people and everything about who they are. If religion were enough, Nicodemus would not have needed to go to Jesus.

The people just described in the New Testament were all held in chains. They were chained by possessions, chained by sexual immortality, chained by sickness, and chained by religious traditions. There are all sorts of things that we allow to constrain us and halt our progress. We often find ourselves in a self-made prison.

There is another biblical character that was in prison and bound by chains.

Do you remember Paul, not Saul, the new man in Christ Jesus, apostle Paul of Acts 16:25–26? Paul and his friend Silas were in jail, bound in chains because they disturbed people's lives and livelihood with the Gospel of Jesus Christ. Sometimes we can get tangled up in the chains of others. Paul and Silas were in the jailhouse with other chained-up folks. The Bible did not give an explanation relative to why the other people were in chains. Maybe they were chained by holding on to anger, hatred, depression, fear, unforgiveness, jealousy, worry, bitterness, or grief that resulted in their self-made prisons. Look what happened. "The prison doors flew open, and everybody's chains came loose." Every chain was broken. They were no longer bound. The power of God can break every chain.

Monk and spiritual writer Albert Holtz relates a story of wandering the streets of Toledo, Spain, and encountering an interesting sight at the monastery church of San Juan de Los Reyes. Way up on the outside wall in neat rows were curious ironwork objects about a foot and a half long. They were ankle chains taken off Christian slaves freed from their Muslim captors who ruled this Spanish city for over 360 years (until liberated by the Spaniards in 1492). Holtz suggest that these chains are most appropriate hanging on the monastery church.[27] For Holtz, the broken chains were appropriate trophies for us Christians, since it showed our former sin captivity. God loosed our bonds by becoming flesh. He died, was buried, and arose freeing all humanity from the chains of sin that enslaved us. After all, God is in the business of breaking chains.

Why remain chained to the things from which Christ died to set us free? We aren't dogs and don't have to be chained. At the name of Jesus, every chain is broken.

Philippians 2:10–11 tells us, "At the name of Jesus every knee should bow ... and that every tongue should confess that Jesus Christ is Lord, to the glory of God the Father." There is power in the name of Jesus, and He is the best chain-breaker ever. What must you do? I'm so glad you asked. Where there is sin, repent. Where bitterness, anger, and hate have taken root, forgive those you have aught against and forgive yourself. Break the chains that have you in prison all tied up. If there is anything that is holding you down, break those chains in the name of Jesus. There is power in the name of Jesus! Jesus is in the business of breaking chains. Because of His blood, we have new life in Jesus Christ and the "chains that bind" can't hold us anymore. Because of Jesus, you can shout, "Free at last! Jesus has broken my chains! I'm coming out! Hallelujah! Praise the Lord! I'm free."

You have the chance to see those chains broken in your life, and you can start a new life.

If you haven't accepted Jesus as your personal Savior, do it now. Jesus longs to start a relationship with you. He wants to break the chains in your life and give you a freedom you have never experienced before. If you have accepted Christ but remain chained to something that is not of God, allow Christ to set you free today through rededicating yourself to Him. Christ wants you to experience faith, not religion.

Christ wants each of us to experience true life that only can be found in Him. Today, chains can be broken. The question is this: are you willing to let Christ break your chains?

> "He brought them out of darkness and the shadow of death, and brake their bands in sunder. Oh, that men would praise the LORD for His goodness, and for His wonderful works to the children of men! For He hath broken the gates of brass, and cut the bars of iron in sunder." -Psalm 107:14–16 (KJV)

CONCLUSION

Psalmist Malisa Davis, in her poem "Break These Chains," said to God,

> "Break these chains that bind me, Lord. Break these chains and release my destiny. I am forever safe in Your arms. I will soar on Your winds of love and proclaim the wonders of Your love. Your love will set me free."[28]

Each day is a fresh start for you to be free in Jesus' name.

Notes

27. Holtz, Albert. *Pilgrim Road: A Benedictine Journey through Lent*, Harrisburg, PA, Morehouse Publishing, 2006.
28. Davis, Malisa. *Break These Chains*, San Jose, CA, https://allpoetry.com/6806207-Break-These-Chains-bymalisa101664, 2010.

The War Within

> "I find then a law, that, when I would do good, evil is present with me. For I delight in the law of God after the inward man: But I see another law in my members, warring against the law of my mind, and bringing me into captivity to the law of sin which is in my members."
> —Romans 7:21–23 (KJV)

'"There's a war going on and if you're gonna win you better make sure that you have Jesus deep down within. This battle cannot be won with bullets and guns for the enemy you cannot see with human faculties."[29] This first verse of Walter Hawkins's song describes Ephesians 6:10–18. The war that the followers of Christ Jesus have to fight are with principalities and the rulers of darkness, namely Satan and his imps. We are at war!

It's not easy being a Christian. It's not easy being anybody these days. The economy is in the tank. People are running themselves ragged trying to keep up. Crime is on the rampage. Life here on this earth ain't easy, whether Christian or not. Many believers are unaware of the wars we face daily. There are spiritual wars around us at all times. In addition, there is a whole new set of problems that comes with being a child of the Most High God. This world will mock you, shun you, look down upon you, and call you names. We have to cope with the evils and temptations of our environment that try to lead us astray (i.e., the decline in values by the media, our government enforcing and reinforcing ideas that are contrary to God's Word, and the moral fiber of our country continuing to plummet). The potholes of degradation and evil grow deeper. These are but a few outside forces that encompass Christian life making godly living difficult.

In addition to this continuous outer conflict, there's another war going on which is the war within us. We struggle day and night with the "old self" and the "new self," the "old man" warring against the "new man." There is the "war within" that we have to contend with. The toughest battle you will ever have is the battle within yourself, the battle between who you were, who you are now, and who you want to be. We must fight to win this war with Mr. and Ms. Self. Satan will devour and pick off Christians when they fail to engage in warfare against their own inner voice.

This war within is the conflict inside you which toggles between doing what you know is right and according to God's Word but you don't do. This is what the apostle Paul was saying in Romans 7:18–25. God's Word says it's the wrong way to go but you go ahead anyway. There is a disconnect between your conscience and your actions. God says, "Do this," and you don't. God says, "Don't do that," but you do. No matter how much we may wish to do right, to be righteous, we find ourselves sinning. The apostle Paul described his "wretched man" frustration in Romans 7. Now keep in mind this self-confessed "wretched man" may have been the greatest Christian who ever lived, and if he is a "wretched man," then who are you and I? This paradox of doing what you don't want to do and not doing what you know to do, not doing the good you want to do, but the evil you keep doing. What a tongue twister. Paul is expressing how twisted the human soul is; even the Christian soul can be. It is this weak, pesky, old sinful nature, the flesh that keeps hanging around and doing war with the new person in Christ Jesus.

"Simul Justus et Peccator," is a phrase said by the theologian Martin Luther that is translated as "Righteous and at the same time a Sinner." He further explains that saints are righteous because they believe in Jesus Christ, whose righteousness covers them and is imputed on them. They are sinners because they do not fulfill (obey) the law and are not without sinful desires.[30] Luther describes Christians "simultaneously saint and sinner" because he redefines "saint" as a forgiven sinner. We are called saints not because we changed into something different but because our relationship with God changes as a result of God's grace.[31]

Does this describe you? You believe in Jesus Christ. You know your sins are forgiven by the blood of the Lamb. You know you are heading to heaven, and you know God's commandments are good, right, and the best thing for you, yet you have trouble doing them. Look at Exodus 20:3–17. Let's check out just three or four of them. What about number four, which says, "Remember the Sabbath and keep it holy"? You don't always keep it holy. You skip church every once in a while. I'm talking about times before the COVID pandemic. When you do come to church, you watch the clock and don't take to heart the preached word because what the long-winded preacher is saying is for someone else.

Number six is "Thou shalt not kill." No, you are not a murderer. However, you have hateful thoughts and words and with your killer tongue. You express this hate that will kill the spirit of anyone hearing your killer words.

Commandment number seven is "Thou shalt not commit adultery." You have that hidden porno, you play around, sleep around practicing "love the one you're with" even if they belong to another. We can't forget number nine. "Thou shalt not bear false witness against thy neighbor." You have an attack of *gossipitis,* becoming a cell phone sinner. With this device, you infect the airways tearing down and killing reputations of family, friends, coworkers, neighbors, and yes, Christian brothers and sisters, including the pastor. You know what God said but you do it anyway. Some even try to justify what they know they shouldn't do. What a mess! What a conflict! What a battle with "self"! Christians are stuck on sin in thought, word, and deed.

The "war within" is real and difficult. We do not have to fight it alone. Saints can encourage each other. However, there are those who struggle and suffer in silence. The reasons so many struggle alone is because they don't want others to see their real lives. They put on a mask to guard their hearts. They watch what they say and what they do so people can't see how sinful they really are. In their minds, they are good people. After all, they are Christians, not like "those people." They are holy and righteous. They don't talk about their real struggles. They tend to skirt around the peripheries and rule out their real issues. They do not share their struggles with anyone. I know we must be careful who we share our struggles with and who we confide in. Some folks do have loose lips, and you don't want your struggles discussed on Facebook. In the proper environment, with people you love and trust, and with those who love and trust you, there can be reciprocal help and healing. I had such a friend, God rest her soul, with whom I could tell my struggles. We would share our deep dark secrets with each other. We would pray together and for each other. We would search God's Word for scriptures that we hung on to in order to gain strength for our battles. We were authentic, real with each other, and were the same with our talks with Jesus, our Lord.

Being authentic has power. Satan wants us to live a double life, a hypocritical life. It is the openness of being authentic that give us victory in our lives and in the lives of others. We don't have to play the hypocrite, pretending to be holy when we know we have something wrong down deep inside. We come to God's house Sunday after Sunday, Bible study after Bible study, prayer meeting after prayer meeting, wearing a mask covering the war going on inside us that controls and directs our lives. We don't have to struggle in silence all alone.

In verse 24 of Romans 7 (paraphrased), Paul calls himself a "wretched, miserable man." He asks who will rescue him from this body that brings him not joy but death. Then in verse 25, he gives the answer. "Thank God for His salvation through Jesus Christ our Lord." God delivers us through His Son Jesus Christ.

In Romans 7, according to the KJV, the word "I" is used thirty-two times in the twenty-five verses. The Holy Spirit is not mentioned. The "I" finds only defeat. In Romans 8, instead of the word "I," we find the word "Spirit" used sixteen times. We must yield our lives to Jesus. This is our part. Jesus will fill us with His Spirit. That's Jesus's part. After the "I" has failed in Romans 7, Romans 8 opens with "no condemnations" and ends with "no separation." It's the "I" in sin that must be removed and replaced with "o," and you have "son." The Son of God will give the victory. There is victory in Jesus. We must step out of our self-filled life into a Spirit-filled life.

What do we do? Where do we turn for help? Our efforts of self-improvement or turning over a new leaf will never be enough as we continue to fail. This is no excuse for remaining in a sinful state. We should never give ourselves over to sin, developing reprobate and debased minds doing what ought not to be done. By no means should we forgo resisting the devil's pull of giving up the fight of flesh against spirit. The struggle will always be with us on this side of heaven. We are in real trouble if sin is no longer a struggle. This would mean we have lost the war, lost faith, and have surrendered to the enemy within.

Too many people think that we have great willpower and the ability to conquer our issues and that's where we fail. When our backs are against the wall and we confess to God that we can't make it and we need His help, that's when God says, "I'm coming." The scripture says (Romans 10:11, 13), "Whoever believes on Him will not be put to shame," and "Whoever calls on the name of the LORD shall be saved." What is impossible with man is possible with God. The "war within" can only be conquered by the victory found in Jesus Christ. God's children are safe when Christ surrounds them, the Holy Spirit is within them, and God our Father is for us.

Conclusion

The ultimate victory of the war within is not in us but in Jesus Christ. The God of peace will soon crush Satan under our feet. Victory is ours for the asking and we can tell that old Satan to "get behind." We have the victory in Jesus. Thank God for deliverance that we could not give ourselves. What could not be done in human strength has been done by our Lord and Savior. If it had not been for Jesus and His precious blood, there would be no deliverance. We would not be free from the bondage of sin had it not been for Jesus. "But thanks be to God, which giveth us the victory through our Lord Jesus Christ," says 1 Corinthians 15:57 (KJV).

The apostle Paul says in Galatians 5:16–18 (KJV),

> "This I say then, walk in the Spirit, and ye shall not fulfill the lust of the flesh. For the flesh lusteth against the Spirit, and the Spirit against the flesh: and these are contrary the one to the other: so that ye cannot do the things that ye would. But if ye be led of the Spirit, ye are not under the law."

Walk and live, my brothers and sisters, in the Spirit, and you will have victory in Jesus Christ. Each day is a fresh start for you to move forward in victory.

Notes

29. Hawkins, Walter. "There's a War Going On," *Love Alive III,* Waco, TX, Light Records, Word Records-MNRK Music Group, 1993.
30. Luther, Martin. *The Westminster Confession of Faith, "Of Good Works,"* chapter XVI, v, vi. London-Edinburg, England, Evan Tyler, printer to the King Most Excellent Majesty, 1646–1647.
31. Kleinhans, Kathryn, A. *Saints and Sinners,* Columbus, OH, https://www.livinglutheran.org/2005/04/saints-sinners.

SECTION 4
MY ENEMY IS ME

WHEN YOU CAUSED THE STORM

> "Then said they unto him, what shall we do unto thee, that the sea may be calm unto us? for the sea wrought, and was tempestuous. And he said unto them, take me up, and cast me forth into the sea; so shall the sea be calm unto you: for I know that for my sake this great tempest is upon you."
> —Jonah 1:11–12 (KJV)

Storms are formed when the movements of cold and warm air currents create extreme air pressure differences. Extreme air pressure is created at an atmospheric level as warm, wet air rushes, causing cold air to move toward the area where air pressure is lower, eventually creating a rotation. The rotational movement of cold and warm air in the atmosphere is centered around an area of low air pressure that is surrounded by a high-pressure system. A low and high air pressure system can be generated at a local level as hot air rises off the ground. This creates relatively small air disturbances, such as whirlwinds or dust devils. The type of storm that is generated varies depending on temperature and weather conditions around the system. Cold storm systems can take the shape of an ice storm, blizzard, or snowstorm. In dry or desert areas, firestorms, windstorms, or dust devils can be generated. Storms in tropical areas can take the form of a cyclone or a thunderstorm.[32] These are natural conditions that produce storms on this earth. The question is this: can people cause storms?

In life sometimes the sea is calm and the wind blows softly. There are times when the wind rises, the sky darkens, and we find ourselves in the midst of a terrible storm. There are many different storms in life that we all encounter. Of course, we have nature-producing storms. In the Bible, I found that there are three kinds of storms: storms that God allows for our growth, storms caused by others, and storms that we cause.

Let's briefly examine a growth storm used by God. In Mark 4:35–41, Jesus commanded His disciples to get into a boat and go to the other side of the sea. Jesus knew a storm was brewing and used this bit of adversity to grow and develop His disciples' faith. This may bother the Christians who look for a guarantee of a trouble-free life. In this scripture passage, the disciples did exactly what Jesus had commanded and a great storm arose. They got into their storm by being obedient. They were following the commandments they were given. They got out of their storm when divine authority was exercised by the powerful word of the creator of the wind and water. Jesus said to the storm, "Peace, be still! And the wind ceased and there was a great calm" (Mark 4:39). The disciples' faith increased after they came out of the storm. God will use the University of Adversities to grow and mature us.

Sometimes we are dragged into the storms of other people. Have you ever been negatively affected by the wrongdoings and actions of others? That's where we find the apostle Paul in Acts 27. He was being transported by boat to stand trial in Rome. During this time of year, bad weather for sailing was on the horizon. Being led by the Holy Spirit, Paul gave warning to the men. "Men, I perceive that this voyage will end with disaster and much loss, not only of the cargo and ship, but also our lives. Before very long, a wind of hurricane force, called the 'northeaster,' swept down from the island. The ship was caught by the storm" (Acts 27:10–15). Paul was dragged into a storm by others. Often the actions and disobedience of others will affect us. The actions may not be aimed at you personally, but you can still get caught in the fallout. It is important that we take care not to develop a victim mentality and have a pity party. We must stay free of unforgiveness, resentment, and bitterness. We must look to God to help us do what we can't do and persevere in our faith in God. Paul maintained his enduring faith in God through the storm.

Little spring showers may make life inconvenient. Thunder and lightning may make life difficult, and hurricanes and tornadoes may put life in danger. There are some storms that we cause, storms of our own making. I call the storms we engineer by our own foolishness and disobedience "Jonah storms." In the book of Jonah, chapter 1, we read how Jonah engineered his storm when he tried to run from the presence of God and His instructions. God had given Jonah a very clear assignment. Jonah knew exactly what God wanted him to do. Jonah was to witness to the evil Gentile people of Nineveh. Jonah didn't want any non-Jews ("those people") to obtain God's favor. He made the bad decision to do something different. Most bad decisions we make are because we want to have our own way. We are rebellious and we on purpose, knowingly, choose to make bad decisions.

When we choose to be disobedient, we don't realize we are also choosing the consequences of that disobedience. Then we have the nerve to be surprised when we must reap the fallout that is the consequence of our folly. Jonah was trying to get away from the will of God. Read the whole story and keep this in mind. As Jonah ran from God, he went down, down, down—down to Joppa, down into the ship, and down into the sea and into the belly of a big fish. Jonah was headed in the opposite direction from where God had told him to go. Whenever you are out of the will of God, your direction spirals downward. In verse 10, Jonah tells the others on the ship that he was running from God. Imagine God's prophet running away from God and telling folks that he's running from God. He made a real bad decision. Because of his willful disobedience, Jonah caused a storm.

We often make decisions in haste. We do stuff even when we know it's wrong and against God's Word. Proverbs 19:3 (KJV) says, "The foolishness of man perverteth his way: and his heart fretteth against the Lord." Let me unpack this for you. We ruin our lives by our own foolishness, ignorance, and our own willful neglect of doing the right thing. We refuse to make changes according to God's Word. We deny our sin-problem by wanting to dress it up, making it politically correct and acceptable to Satan's society. This action causes self-made storms. Once in our storm, we have the audacity to blame God and others.

We need to take ownership of our actions. Jonah was not in a state of denial. He knew he had messed up. He admitted he was at fault and that he had caused the storm.

It's your thing. Do what you want to do, but then you've caused a storm, maybe more than one storm. What do you do after you've gotten yourself in a heap of big messes? What should you do when you caused that storm? Be like Jonah. Fess up and sign your name to the storm you caused. Confess you have messed up. The Word says in 1 John 1:9 (KJV), "If we confess our sins, he is faithful and just to forgive us our sins, and to cleanse us from all unrighteousness." God is a Genesis God, a God of new beginnings and in the forgiving business. When something happens and you fall out of the will of God and you have missed the mark, run to God and get back on point. Don't stay out in the storm and rain. Learn from your mistakes and mishaps. God loves you. He wants to help you and not condemn you. Don't run away from God just when you need Him most. You've been in the storm too long. God calms the storms and stills the waves. Don't focus on your storms, self-made or otherwise. Don't let the storm carry you away from the shore or out to sea. Jonah tried to escape from God, but God never left him. We are never out of the sight of God. We can never flee from His presence. God is wherever we are. Even when you've caused the storm, don't hesitate to call on God. Don't allow guilt to keep you away from God.

Following their growth storm, the disciples made it to the other side of the sea. After the storm caused by others, Paul made it to Rome. After Jonah's self-made storm, he made it to Nineveh. Don't let the storms of life distract you from your purpose and the will of God. Keep your eyes focused on God and His Word. Regardless of the source of the storm, God is in every situation. He has sovereign rule of everything. He is the eye of all our storms.

Conclusion

"When the storms of life are raging and the billows are tossing high, the waters are threatening to over flow you, and hope begins to fade away, that's when Jesus intervenes, for He is the guardian of your soul. Saying to your storm "be still." Stand firmly on the solid rock Jesus Christ. For the way of the Lord is a refuge, the righteous run in and are safe."[33]

> Hear the declaration of Jeremiah, "This I recall to my mind, therefore have I hope. It is of the Lord's mercies that we are not consumed, because His compassions fail not. They are new every morning: great is thy faithfulness. The Lord is my portion, saith my soul; therefore will I hope in Him." -Lamentations 3:21–24 (KJV)

Each day is a fresh start for you to move forward in peace.

Notes

[32.] Staff writer. *What Causes Storms,* Oakland, CA, https://Reference.com/Ask Media Group, 2020.

[33.] Mullins, Margaret Christine. *When the Storms of Life Are Ragging,* Freeport, FL, https://www.authorsden.com, 2009.

Three Hard Words: "I Was Wrong"

"And the son said unto him, Father, I have sinned against heaven, and in thy sight, and am no more worthy to be called thy son."
—Luke 15:21 (KJV)

When someone fails to take the responsibility for their mistakes, they try to remove their guilt with one of three methods: run and hide, cover it up, or blame it on someone else. English poet Alexander Pope coined, in part, "To err is human ..."[34] Some say to blame your failure on others is also human. However, it is not God's way. Comedian Flip Wilson became known for his hilarious phrase "The devil made me do it."[35] Rather than take responsibility for our mess-ups, we blame others including our archenemy, Satan.

There's a funny story that I heard many years ago about Satan and the angel Gabriel. It seems that Satan was sitting on the curb outside a megachurch crying. Gabriel asked, "Hey Satan, why the tears? Why are you crying?" Satan replied, through copious tears and sobs, "Those people in that church are telling lies on me. I didn't make them do all that stuff." People routinely lie to hide their sin and their wrongdoing. When they do get caught, they confess as little as possible.

It is very difficult for some to come to the place of total honesty with others, ourselves, or God. For most, it's a continual battle to be transparent in all our dealings. It seems to be easier to cover up or hide our mess-ups. We live in a culture of victimization that gives rewards for blaming others. People are quick to say, "It's their fault. They made me do it. Or the devil made me do it." It's easy to say, "Well, everyone is doing it. Everyone cheats. Everyone lies a little bit. Everyone cheats on their spouse. Everybody uses bad language. Everybody breaks promises now and then." And the list goes on. We live in a society that encourages us to make excuses; however, most people don't need any encouragement in this field.

We are born knowing how to pass the buck. It all goes back to the Garden of Eden in Genesis 3. The serpent came to Eve and tricked her into eating the forbidden fruit. Eve offered some to Adam, and he did eat knowing full well the consequences of his actions because God had told him what would happen (Genesis 2:15–17). When Adam and Eve heard God walking in the garden, they hid. Disobedience had changed everything. Once they walked with God freely. Now this has been replaced with hiding in the forest of their sin. God comes on the scene. Adam is cornered, caught red-handed with a mouth full of the sweet aftertaste of the forbidden fruit. Adam does what many usually do. He passes the buck. In fact, he passes the buck twice. First, in verse 12, Adam blames God, saying, "The woman whom You gave to be with me …" In that same verse, Adam blames Eve, saying, "She gave me of the tree, and I ate." In my imagination, I can hear Adam saying, "Lord, it was all her fault. See what happened was she gave me the fruit and I ate it. What was I supposed to do? Say no and watch her pout all night? And anyway, you put her in the Garden. She wasn't my idea. I'm not complaining, Lord, because she is really beautiful, but I didn't have a problem when it was just me and the animals."

So it goes, the first man and father of the human race is also the first to pass the buck, to shift the blame. This first sin led to the first cover-up. This first wrongdoing led to the first denial. In thousands of years, nothing has really changed. Human nature is still the same. At that point, Adam established the pattern of disobedience, which leads to guilt, which leads to shame, which leads to fear and hiding, which leads to blame shifting, not confessing, and saying those three hard words. "I was wrong."

It states in Proverbs 28:13 (KJV), "He that covereth his sins shall not prosper: but whoso confesseth and forsaketh them shall have mercy." The person who can say, "I was wrong," is on their way to spiritual health. When we sin, we have two options. Option 1 is to conceal it, to cover it up, make excuses, rationalize, or pass the buck. When this happens, we do not prosper. We go through the internal torment of living with a guilty conscience, hoping no one finds us out. In the words of King David (Psalm 32:3 KJV), "When I kept silence, my bones waxed old through my roaring all the day long." We suffer, physically, mentally, and spiritually when we conceal our sins and damage our relationship with God.

Option 2 is to confess our sins and repent of them. Both words—*confess* and *repent*—are important. To confess is to own up to what you have done or did not do. When you confess, you are saying, "Yes, I did it and I know I was wrong." To repent of or to renounce your sins means taking the necessary steps to break the destructive patterns and/or habits in your life. When you do this, you are saying, "I've been walking down the wrong path, and now with the help of God's Holy Spirit, I'm going to change directions."

"I was wrong" are not easy words to say. As long as you don't admit you're wrong, you can't be forgiven, relationships will remain broken, and you will struggle with bitterness and anger and remain locked out of the abundant life Jesus came to provide. Without forgiveness, your life will remain broken, fragmented, and you will never know holiness, wholeness, good mental health, or spiritual health.

In Luke 15, Jesus told a story about a young man who felt the urge to leave his father's house. It's a familiar story. Allow me to paraphrase and give this story a modern flavor.

This young man asked for his portion of the family estate. After receiving his father's hard-earned money, he left for a distant land. There he squandered his money on wild living and pseudofriends. Days passed. The day came when the young man had spent all his money. Now penniless and destitute, he found himself in a desperate place far from home, family, and true friends. He was ashamed and hired on with a farmer who put him to work slopping hogs. He was so hungry that he found himself ready to eat with the pigs.

At that precise moment, the light turned on in his brain. In a blinding flash, he saw himself. He realized that his willfulness and irresponsibility got him in this mess. In the moment of self-revelation, he saw what he had become. He knew he was wrong and that there was only one way back. The irony of his situation hit him like a ton of bricks. His father's servants were eating some real good food while he, the master's son, and a Jew, was living with pigs. Again, a flash of light. "I'm going home." "When I get there, I'm going to say, 'Father, I have sinned against heaven and against you. I am no longer worthy to be called your son; make me like one of your hired men.'" With that, the young man got up, brushed himself off, gathered his things, and began making the long journey home.

He was still a long way off when his father spotted him trudging up the dusty road. Before the young man knew what was happening, his father ran to him, threw his arms around him, and kissed him, saying, "Welcome home, son."

The son said what he had memorized in the pigpen. "Father, I have sinned against you and against heaven. I am no longer worthy to be called your son." He didn't get to say, "Make me a hired servant," because his father cut him off and said to his servants, "Quick! Bring the best robe and put it on him. Put a ring on his finger and sandals on his feet. Bring the fattened calf and kill it. Let's have a feast and celebrate. For this son of mine was dead and is alive again; he was lost and is found."

This young man, whom we know as the prodigal son, turned his life around by saying six hard words. "I have sinned. I was wrong." He said it while he was still broke and hungry, while he was still living with the pigs, and while he was still a long way from home. This may be a parable of your life. When we have messed up, we are so ashamed to find ourselves in the pigpen that we dare not tell anyone where we are, so we suffer silently. We try to make ourselves presentable, brush our teeth and comb our hair, but we still of have pig slop under our fingernails. Down deep in the pores of our epidermis lingers the smell of pigs, and the best cologne can't kill the smell.

This story is for everyone who is tired of being with the pigs. If you are ready to give up, admit your wrong, and really come home, I've got good news for you. God, your heavenly Father, is standing in the road waiting for you with open arms. He knows where you've been. Nothing is hidden from Him, and He still loves you, in spite of your past. The only thing that matters is for you to come home. That's what grace and mercy are all about. With God's grace, you get what you *don't* deserve. With God's mercy, you *don't* get what you do deserve. You can come home. You can start over. You can be forgiven. Your slate will be wiped clean. You don't have to live the rest of your life hiding and suffering silently. All you have to say is "Father, God, I've sinned. I was wrong." When you do, you will find that there is joy in being wrong because God is full of grace, mercy, and forgiveness. God's Word says in 1 John 1:9 (KJV), "If we confess our sins, he is faithful and just to forgive us our sins, and to cleanse us from all unrighteousness." I pray that you have the courage to say these three hard words: "I was wrong."

Conclusion

As long as you refuse to admit you've done anything wrong, you can never experience God's forgiveness. Your refusal to own up to your sin means you will live with the burden of your past hanging like a millstone around your neck. You will stay just like you are right now, unforgiven, unhealthy, fragmented, broken, confused, divided, locked inside the stronghold of your own self-denial and self-deception. "I was wrong." These three words can change your life. The lyrics to a song recorded by Donnie Harper and the New Jersey Mass Choir sums up the changes we are able to make in our lives.

It's In Jesus

"I have found a love that pardons. I have found some stripes that heal. I have found strength for my weakness. I have found grace to cover all my sins. It's in Jesus, only Jesus. It's in Jesus He's the One. Rock of salvation, a strong foundation, it's in Jesus, He is the One."[36]

Each day is a fresh start for you to move forward in the truth of God's Word.

Notes

34. Pope, Alexander. *An Essay on Criticism, Part 2,* London, EN, https://www.phrases.org.UK, Kessinger Publishing, 2004 (first published 1711).
35. Wilson, Clerow "Flip" Jr. *The Devil Made Me Buy This Dress Album,* New York, https://en.Wikipedia.org/the_flip_wilson_show, Little David Records, NBC, 1979.
36. Harper, Donnie, New Jersey Mass Choir. *Hope of the World*: *It's in Jesus*, Pittsburgh, https://www.hoperecords.com, Hope Records, 1992.

Section 5
Lord, Help Me

Coping with Grief and Loss

> "Blessed be God, even the Father of our Lord Jesus Christ, the Father of mercies, and the God of all comfort; Who comforteth us in all our tribulation, that we may be able to comfort them which are in any trouble, by the comfort wherewith we ourselves are comforted of God".
> —2 Corinthians 1:3–5 (KJV)

It is amazing how God orchestrates events in our lives to meet our every need. As I begin to present this section of my dissertation, "Grief and Loss," I am in the midst of experiencing grief and loss. Not that this is my first encounter with grief, but at this particular time, it's very fresh. I've just lost a very dear friend of mine, and to compound my grief, my friend died on the same day my son, Howard, died twenty-one years ago. It seems that God arranges a distraction around this time every year to take my attention off my pain so that I can focus on others and be a very present help to them. It's as if God says to me, "OK, LaRuth, there's no time for a pity party. Howard is with me and I have a new assignment for you." I have experienced firsthand the comforting presence and power of God. God comforts me so that I may extend comfort to others.

When we hear the word *grief,* we immediately think of death. However, we experience grief in several ways, such as the loss of a job, loss of status, prized possessions, a pet, a body part, health, youth, independence, and divorce. We call this tangible grief. There is also intangible grief. This is when we lose someone in a physical or emotional way but they have not necessarily died (i.e., a family member or friend who is physically absent but not psychologically present). Examples include a soldier missing in action not found dead or alive, a kidnapped victim, and a runaway child, one who is suddenly away and there is little hope of their return. Then there is the opposite (i.e., a family member or friend who is physically present but psychologically absent). Examples are Alzheimer's, dementia, or stroke victims suffering progressive loss of mental and intellectual capabilities. No matter what the loss may be, grief is real.

What is grief? Grief is the pain we feel when we lose someone or something very special to us. Grief is intense sorrow. Sorrow is mental distress caused by loss or disappointment. Sorrow is heartbreak, sadness, and afflictions. Grief and sorrow are tangled balls of emotions. This includes loneliness, fear, anxiety, confusion, emptiness, anger, guilt, depression, bitterness, relief, and the list goes on. The depth of grief depends on the relationship with the person or prized possessions. Grief and loss can be overwhelming. The balanced life we once had has tilted and we are caught off-centered.

In Elisabeth Kübler-Ross's book *Death and Dying*, she noted that the terminally ill experienced five stages of accepting death. She listed them as denial/isolation, anger, bargaining, depression, and acceptance. The one thing that persists with all these stages is hope.[37] Similarly to the stages experienced by the Kübler-Ross study are the stages of grief. These eight stages are noted in Wiersbe and Wiersbe's book *Comforting the Bereaved*. These grief stages are shock, strong emotion, depression, fear, guilt, anger, apathy, and adjustment.[38] These stages of grief come in no particular order. They come and go randomly. Just when we think we are all right, we're not. It's like swinging on a pendulum, sometimes up and sometimes down. It is also important to remember that the grieving process has no time limit and there is no right or wrong way to grieve. Grieving is individual to the person and the relationship. If there has been no contact with Uncle Joe for ten or twenty years, you may not have experienced strong emotional grief. But if Uncle Joe has been in your life and has been a significant part of your life for ten or twenty years, then your grief might be deep and emotional.

These feelings and emotions are quite normal when one is grieving. The ability to recognize these feelings helps to support the grieving process. To acknowledge and accept the loss is the first step to bring balance back to our lives. Realize that by feeling your pain you are actually healing. Death and grief are universal. We all will have to cope with bereavement, grief, and loss at some stage of life. These patterns and behaviors sound logical and understandable. But is there a biblical basis for them? Did anyone in the Bible experience these stages of grief?

There is an interesting parallel between stages of grief and the experience of Jeremiah as recorded in Lamentations, which is known as the "Book of Years" and the funeral song for Jerusalem. Lamentations reveals Jeremiah's grief over the fall of Jerusalem. It is a series of five elegies (poems of mourning) expressing grief that weighs heavily on the heart of Jeremiah. Jeremiah described Jerusalem as a woman that has been reduced to widowhood. He grieves because of the devastation of God's chosen people who were killed, tortured, and taken captive. The prophet is expressing his grief through this descriptive song of sorrow. We find some stages of the grieving process in chapter 1 of Lamentations and the following verses. In verse 2, we read of tears and no comfort; verse 3, unrest; verse 4, bitterness; verse 12, great sorrow and sadness; verses 20–22, distress, heartache, and faintheartedness. The fact that Jeremiah expressed these deep emotions of grief in the inspired Word of God indicates that God expects us to grieve and accepts our expressions of grief.

Not everyone progresses through the grief process at the same rate. Grief is unique, and like growth, we cannot rush the process. It takes time and involves pain. Broken hearts have to heal, and healing will come if allowed. Living through grief is work—hard work. Dr. Alan D. Wolfelt stated that love and grief are very much alike. They have power to change our lives. We must surrender to love and must surrender to grief.[39]

We must surrender to our grief. We must work through our grief. When we fail to do grief work, trying to avoid the process or suffer silently, we only harm our spirits, bodies, minds, and souls.

There are some physical and mental conditions associated with grief. Like the stages of grief, there are symptoms of grief. Some physical symptoms are weight gain/loss, headaches, insomnia, gastrointestinal disorders, excessive sleeping, health symptoms of the deceased, and becoming accident prone. Some mental symptoms include fear, depression, being suicidal, being disoriented, frustration, and preoccupation with belongings of the deceased. There are also some behavioral symptoms that warrant attention (i.e., withdrawal, change in appearance, poor hygiene, decrease in self-care, use of alcohol and drugs, and using grief to legitimize bad behavior).

During a counseling session, it was noted how a Christian counselee used her grief as an excuse to be verbally abusive. Her excuse would be "Well, you know I'm grieving my mother's death." It was also noted that her mother had been dead fifteen years, and the counselee also used this excuse as a manipulative tool to get what she wanted. The counselor reminded her that regardless of any situation, she was still accountable to God for her behavior. She gave her a homework assignment to study and write the meaning of Philippians 1:27 (KJV), which states, "Only let your conversation be as it becometh the gospel of Christ …" This assignment also included Philippians 2:3–5 (KJV). "Let nothing be done through strife or vainglory; but in lowliness of mind let each esteem other better than themselves. Look not every man on his own things, but every man also on the things of others. Let this mind be in you, which was also in Christ Jesus."

With work and prayer, the counselee mended her ways and asked for forgiveness from those she had offended and God. We cannot delay grief. It will not go away by itself. It is vital to our wellbeing to surrender to our grief. Unresolved grief is like a festering sore covered by a superficial scar. It will spread and infect all your whole life and the lives of those around you.

We must move beyond our grief, and we don't have to feel guilty about it. As in life, growth is a process. Grief is a process and as we go through it we can grow through it. To hide our pain and suffer in silence allows for self-destruction. Facing our pain and embracing our grief starts the process of healing. Even in seemingly negative experiences of life, grief is healthy and good. Yes, there is such a thing as "good grief"! We don't have to be stuck or become stagnate in grief and sorrow.

The Bible has several examples of those who went from grief to growth and action. In Genesis 50, Joseph wept after the loss of his father Jacob. In verses 15–21, Joseph forgave and comforted his brothers for the evil they had done to him. Joseph went from grief to forgiveness, comfort, and help. In Nehemiah 1:1–11, the prophet cried, mourned, and fasted because of his grief. However, he turned from grief to praise, thanksgiving, repentance, and seeking to improve the situation. Job, in chapters 1 and 13, was overwhelmed by grief and loss but he did not abandon hope or trust in God. He went from grief to worship and trust. In Matthew 14, after the death of His cousin, John the Baptist, Jesus sought solitude to be alone with His grief. He didn't stay there. He did not dwell on His grief. He returned to His ministry. Jesus went from grief to ministry. We can learn and grow through grief and loss. Working through grief allows for growth as we depend on and trust in God. God is in our grief. He can resurrect us from grief and lift us up to a new life and future. No! It won't be the same. With the help of God's Holy Spirit, it can be good.

We can work through the healing process by:

- not ignoring our feelings (It is OK to cry.)
- accepting the reality of our loss (We cannot change what has happened.)
- knowing healing cannot be rushed (It takes time and patience.)
- adjusting to a new environment (Set short-term goals.)
- reinvesting yourself in a productive way (Share with, care for, and comfort others.)
- realizing that everyone faces losses and you are not alone
- seeking help (It is all right for a child of God to seek Christian counseling. Do not reject the help that God sends you.)
- above all, consider God

God is in your grief. Open yourself and your feelings up to Him who is able to keep you from falling and waiting to bring you healing and comfort. God has given us a great resource, His power! He called this world into existence with a three-letter word. "Let." From the day of creation, the sun still shines by day and the moon by night. The stars are still suspended in the sky, and this earth still rotates around the sun. That's power! Through your grief and loss, God, Elohim, your creator and sustainer, can and will keep you. When deep sorrow fills your heart, when your eyes with tears grow dim, when the hope within you dies and your dreams are shattered into pieces, and when your cup of grief overflows, then consider Him. God is the mender of broken hearts, minds, and spirits. Leave all your needs to Him. God is omnipotent, omniscient, omnipresent, and forever love.

Conclusion

The death of a loved one or any significant loss in life can test our faith and shake our world, turning it upside down. Working through grief and its roller-coaster rides is hard work. Much like healing from a physical injury, death and loss leave a wound, a scar. Physical wounds will heal. The pain will ease, but the mark of the scar will remain. Healing will return little by little. Our life will not be the same; however, it will continue. Our life is not over, only different. We must forge ahead carrying our memories of our loss and meet the new challenges of life. Death and loss bring about changes and change is a part of life. We are never the same. We are either better or bitter. We either sink or swim. It's our choice. Managing these intrusions in our lives requires action on our part. We must become directly involved in our own healing process.

During a period of rehabilitation, the demands of physical therapy are uncomfortable, even painful. For example, knee replacement surgery will not heal unless the pain of therapy is accepted and the tasks of healing are achieved. Likewise, our grief and loss therapy calls for acceptance of our pain and the need to accomplish the healing task. This lets us know that our broken hearts, minds, and spirits need mending. And who can do this better than our heavenly Father? Psalm 34:17–18 (NIV) tells us, "The righteous cry out, and the Lord hears them; He delivers them from all their troubles. The Lord is close to the brokenhearted and saves those who are crushed in spirit."

Noted philosopher and theologian Nicholas Wolterstorff, who was mourning the death of his son, expressed his grief in his book entitled *Lament for a Son*. Though this passage is quite personal, Wolterstorff decided to publish it in hope that it will be of help to some of those who find themselves with us company of mourners.

"To believe in Christ's rising and death's dying is also to live with the power and the challenge to rise up now from our graves of suffering love. If sympathy for the world's wounds is not enlarged by our anguish; if gratitude for what is good does not flame up; if insight is not deepened; if commitment to what is important is not strengthened; if aching for a new day is not intensified; if hope is weakened and faith diminished; if from the experience of death comes nothing good, the death has won."[40]

We can't let death win. Death can't win and does not have the final say. Jesus took care of that. When He returns, death will be no more and He shall wipe all tears away. In the meantime, in the in-between time, in the dash between life and death, keep the faith and keep trusting in the one who is able to keep you by His divine power.

Because of the sin of Adam, we are confronted with death. God made man to live and not die. When Adam and Eve sinned, death walked in. Romans 5:12 (KJV paraphrased) says, "When Adam sinned, sin entered the entire human race. His sin spread death throughout all the world, so everything began to grow old and die, for all sinned."

We are confounded by death. Death is painful and confusing. We lose loved ones and relationships. They are gone from our sight. One day we will lose ourselves to death. Hallelujah, we are comforted by death. We have the greatest comforter of all, God our heavenly Father. Through His Son, Jesus Christ, death does not have the final word. This earthly death opens the doorway to our eternal life. We exit this world in order to enter our final destination. We are confronted by death. We are confounded by death. All praises be to God, we are comforted by death by God Himself.

Each day is a fresh start for you to trust Jesus all the way.

Notes

37. Kübler-Ross, Elisabeth. *Death and Dying,* New York City, NY, Macmillan Publishing Co., 1969.
38. Wiersbe, Warren W. and Wiersbe, David W. *Comforting the Bereaved*, Chicago, IL, Moody Press, 1985.
39. Wolfelt, Alan D. *The Journey through Grief: Reflections on Healing,* Fort Collins, CO, Center for Loss and Life Transition, Companion Press, 1997.
40. Wolterstorff, Nicholas. *Lament for a Son,* p. 92, Grand Rapids, MI, William B Eerdmans Publishing Co., 1987.

Coping with Health Issues

> "My flesh and my heart faileth: but God is the strength of my heart, and my portion forever."
> —Psalm 73:26 (KJV)

When we are young, health, good health, is often taken for granted. We feel that we are invincible and nothing can happen to us. But stuff happens and we lose our vitality and health. Sickness and disease are facts of life on this sin-filled earth on which we live. Poor health will impact many areas of your life. These interruptions may be temporary or permanent. Coping with illness can be stressful.

Many health conditions are transmitted from animals to humans. Some are the result of our own bad behavior, and others may be genetic in origin. Whatever the cause of our ill health, we need to actively fight, mentally and spiritually, the sickness we are faced with. In case of behavioral causes, we need to survey our lifestyle by checking to see if we are engaging in vices, people, places, or things that tend to contribute to our decline in health.

Transmitted diseases are usually handled with antidotes, serums, and vaccines such as during the COVID-19 outbreak. We can aid in the prevention of disease transmission by practicing hand washing, cleaning contaminated areas and objects, wearing a mask, and practicing safe sex.

Many health issues may be genetically inherited. In this case, we should explore our family medical history to ascertain our susceptibility to the condition, its onset, diagnosis, and prognosis. We should find out all we can about the disease and perhaps undergo genetic screening.

Many people may have all the symptoms of a serious illness but out of fear refuse to get medical help. They procrastinate, not wanting to face reality, and do not seek medical attention. Some even reach way outside the box looking for an instant cure or a catch-all miracle fix. In the meantime, the clock is ticking and the disease is progressing. A correct diagnosis and testing are required for most serious conditions. After accurate diagnosis is received, find as much information as you can about the health problem (i.e., the prescribed treatment plan, side effects of the prescribed medications, costs, and prognosis after treatment). You should take an active part in the decision-making for your treatment and recovery. This means you need to have some basic knowledge of the disease. You don't have to have a medical background, but at least you will have enough moxie to ask questions. Above anyone else, your body is yours and your responsibility.

Dr. Bernie Siegel, in his book *Love, Medicine and Miracles*, explains what he calls the "exceptional patient."[41] Our society paints patients as victims. Exceptional patients refuse to be victims. They become specialists in their care by educating themselves of their illness. They become their own advocates because they want to understand their treatment and participate in it. Included in this is the demand for dignity, personhood, and control no matter what the course of the disease. It takes courage to be exceptional.

According to the Centers for Disease Control, the top ten causes of death and health issues in the US are heart disease, cancer, lung disease, accidents, strokes, Alzheimer's, diabetes, flu and pneumonia, kidney disease, and suicide.[42] Of this list, I am personally familiar with cancer. I am a 40 year breast cancer survivor.

Cancer is part of my paternal family's history. Most of them had some type of cancer. There's a history of cancerous cardiac tumors, lymphosarcoma, gastrointestinal cancer, brain tumors, lung cancer, and breast cancer. Although there was no genetic test for a muted gene, I believe my father's family carried such a gene. My paternal grandparents and great-grandparents lived to ripe old ages (one lived to one hundred and another to 104); however, they left this earth with some type of cancer.

In 1972, I had the honor of caring for my grandmother who was diagnosed with lymphosarcoma, (cancer of the lymphatic system). This type of cancer was hard to diagnose. There was copious testing, and x-rays were required. My grandmother was not your ordinary patient, and she was a pathology assistant. She took a very active part in her diagnosis. She was able to ask questions and help with research of her own tissue samples. She would come home and give me all the details. When her health rapidly began to fail, I took over her care, her questions, and her travel back and forth to medical appointments. I must give the medical staff credit. They never failed to answer my questions or concerns in a dignified manner. They also trained me to administer my grandmother's pain medication, although she never asked for it.

During that time, doctors were known for making house calls. Maybe my grandma got the VIP treatment because she was so well-known at the hospital and I was in line to catch the good fallout. Nevertheless, we both benefited from being active in her health decisions and care. After my grandma's death, I was deemed the family caregiver.

It was in 1982 that I was diagnosed with breast cancer. Because of my grandma's training, I was what Dr. Siegel called an "exceptional patient." Because of my prior knowledge of cancer, my family history, and just plain curiosity, I took a very active part in body care. I'd check for lumps and bumps that were not normal for me. I followed the guidelines of self-breast examination. As providence would have it, I found a lump. This lump didn't feel like the previous ones I had found. So to the doctor I went. He performed all the necessary tests and biopsy. They came back positive for adenocarcinoma. We decided on surgery to remove the breast. Notice I said "we." My doctor gave me choices, but because of my family history, I insisted on a total mastectomy. Before surgery, I asked the doctor to give me time to pray to the Master Physician. I had to pray for him and me. The doctor looked at me strangely as I took his hands. I simply told him he was about to cut on the King's kid and I had to pray for his hands. So I prayed to the Master Physician, my God, asking for guidance, healing, and to let my healing glorify Him. Don't you know my God delivered? After the surgery and the pathology report came back, there was no need for chemotherapy or radiation. We had gotten the cancer in time.

Now there was another issue. What about breast reconstruction? I was just forty-four years old and didn't want to walk around lopsided. In comes the plastic surgeon, and we discussed my options. The doctor and I prayed. It seemed that it had gotten around the hospital that I prayed for my surgeon. The plastic surgeon was expecting me to pray for him too. After the reconstruction, they said my blood count was low and I would need about two units of blood. I asked the nurse to give me until the next day because I had to pray. That night I prayed. The next morning, the lab tech came in to draw blood. That afternoon, the report came back and the units of blood were canceled. Once again, God delivered. Within ten days, I had three surgical procedures and was on my way home.

Do you remember in my prayer for my first surgeon I asked for guidance, healing, and to let my healing glorify Him (God)? After leaving the hospital, I received a call from Karmanos Cancer Society in Detroit requesting me to be a representative for them. I would be a speaker at various breast cancer workshops to encourage women to self-breast examine and to encourage women coping with the effects of breast cancer. Be careful. Don't ask God for something you aren't truly willing to do.

How did I cope with breast cancer? It's called faith, trust, and prayer. I learned from my two grandmothers about having faith and trusting God in all that you say and do. I know sometimes things get tight and you can't seem to get a prayer out. This is the time when you call on a praying friend to intercede for you. Prayer does change things and can also change you in the midst of your situations. In praying for God's healing, be willing to experience healing in the order God sees fit. Psalm 103:3 says, "God is He who forgives all your iniquities, who heals all your disease."

Above all, try to stay positive and focus on those things that are uplifting. It won't be easy, especially when you have intense pain. Be assured that our Savior, Jesus Christ, identifies with our pain and intercedes for us with God, His Father, on our behalf. Stay encouraged.

Around 1999/2000, the American Cancer Society and Karmanos Cancer Society asked women to share their stories about their breast cancer to encourage themselves and others. The following is what I submitted and often used as an introduction to many breast cancer workshops:

Goodbye, My Love[43]

"I don't know how I'm going to live without you. You've been with me so many years. I remember when you and your twin first appeared, so small and delicate. You were all round and firm, and oh so beautiful. You grew to your predetermined size and were the envy of all around. I remember holding you up so high for all to see and admire. I was so proud of you and your twin. Now strangers tell me that I must rid myself of you all because of a small defect you possess. How can I give you up? How can I let go of one so much a part of me, one that makes me so much a woman? I don't want to lose you, my love, my joy, but in the very depths of my soul, I know what I must do.

In the morning, my love, they will come for you. The strangers will come in their sterile scrubbing greens and sharp instruments to take you from me. Within the hour, you'll be gone, gone forever, never to return to this world. Never again will I caress you or see your pointed profile in the mirror. I can no longer keep you near my heart. Of course, your twin will remain to comfort me. But it just won't be the same. You two were the perfect pair. We were the perfect trio. What will life be without you? Those in their sterile scrubs say, "You're no good for me now that your beauty has been spoiled."

I hear your arguments. What will others say? How will I look without you? Well, really, dearest, you know I don't give a hoot about what others think. This is between you, me, and God. You belong to me and God, not to those with narrow minds and tunnel vision. This is about life, my life. And as for appearance, you, my love, can be replaced. Although your replacement will not be as gorgeous as you, it will aesthetically serviceable. The bottom line is I can live without you, you can't live without me, and I can't live with you. I'll still be very much a woman since you are not my total being. There is more to me than just you. I can't and won't sacrifice the whole of me for a small part of me.

The hour is now at hand. They've come for you. Go bravely, my love, and go with faith. God is with us in this our time of sorrow. He hasn't forgotten how precious you are to me. Go, my love, to your new world, and join the others that have preceded you. I'll cherish your memory. Goodbye for now. I'll see you in the great morning when we shall rise and be rejoined in our incorruptible body."[43]

Conclusion

Health issues aren't fun. What is most important is to remain positive and look forward with confidence as you take on this new challenge. Your life may change, but know that your health issue doesn't change who you are. Any health crises will challenge the strongest faith. You are not alone. God is in the midst of all your health issues. Keep the faith, and keep trusting in the power of Almighty God.

> Blessed Heavenly Father,
>
> Many, because of ill health and ravaging pain, have become weak in their faith. Many feel like giving up and quitting the fight. Please, Lord, uphold them with Your powerful hand. Grant them more faith, endurance faith, to stand on Your healing promises that they may experience wholeness and restoration in their bodies. Help them have a deeper trust and hope in You. Bring them comfort and deliverance that only You can give. I exalt Your holy name and give You all the glory. In the name of Jesus, the Christ, I pray and believe. Amen.

Each day is a fresh start for you to trust Jesus for your healing.

Notes

41. Siegel, Bernie S. *Love, Medicine and Miracles,* New York City, NY, Harper and Row Publishers, 1986.
42. Shmerling, Robert H. *Top Ten Causes of Death,* Boston, MA, Harvard Publishing, Harvard Medical School, 2016.
43. Jefferson, LaRuth E. *Goodbye, My Love: Recipes for Hope,* Detroit, MI, Sprint PCS, 2000.

Section 6
Overcoming Failure

I'VE FAILED

> "The Lord upholdeth all that fall, and raiseth
> up all those that be bowed down."
> —Psalm 145:14 (KJV)

No matter how good we are or how successful we may appear to be, we all have failed at something in life. Some of our blunders are small and may go unnoticed. Others may be as large as the Grand Canyon and can be seen by everyone.

We travel in this world with heavy, loaded bags that God never intended for us to carry. In one of those bags are our failures, times when we fell down because we missed the mark. In a game of darts, the object is to hit the bull's-eye dead center. Some of us land our darts on the outer edges of the bull's-eye, missing the center. Others might hit way outside the perimeter of the bull's-eye. Regardless of the distance from the center of the bull's-eye, we've missed the intended mark. We've failed in our attempt to hit the center of the bull's-eye. We carry the guilt of our mistakes in giant bags labeled "Failures." We need to let go of those bags of guilt. We fell down, but we need not stay down. We need not wallow in our failures. We must get up and keep going. We must face our giants.

Max Lucado, in his book *Facing Our Giants,* speaks of life's slump gun.[44] A special gun with a zoom scope. It fires sadness, takes away smiles, and damages our faith. When skies darken, billows roll, and clouds hide the sunshine. When crying is your new occupation and you lose your joy, my friend, you've been slumped by life's slump gun.

Failure is part of our existence. We will not always win the game. We may fail many, many times at many, many things (marriage, parenting, school, business, etc.). Failure, in any particular area, does not mean you are a failure. It means you have room to improve. It gives you another chance, a new beginning, room for new growth, and can lead to success. Failure can be a great teacher. As we learn from our mistakes, we can become successful.

My mother wrote a piece entitled "Successful Attainment." My siblings found it among her papers as we were preparing for her funeral service. We don't know the actual date it was written. It was in her own handwriting and signed by her. We read it at her funeral on April 25, 2009, as part of her legacy to the family. Since it speaks of failure and success, I would like to share parts of it with you.

Successful Attainment[45]

"A calm, useful, and content life contributes to success for everyone. It is not given to one to be a success and another to be a failure. God had given us all we need to be a human being. In order to become successful, we must think successfully. This is a sure fact. We must first allow the successful idea to be born within. We do not want to use the expression "I can't do this" or "I can't do that" because this paralyzes our efforts and our self-confidence. It stops us and blocks us off. Our motivation is lowered and the successful approach is hindered. I feel to be a successful individual, we should use the "I can" pattern often.

When we think success, we have no room for defeat in our minds. We are really making room for the successful thought to come in. We are growing mentally. We are moving toward success. Being successful does not mean having great possessions or lots of money. It means rendering service to others, as well as to ourselves, and living constructively. Not only ought we *think* success, but ought to *talk*. This shows that we believe in success. Let us act successful too. I do not mean that we should pretend or, as we say, "put on." This would be false. If we are going to *think* success, *talk* success, then we are going to attract success, which will automatically cause us to act successfully. With this, we are more apt to find ourselves becoming the successful person we want to be.

Let us keep in mind that God never intended for anybody to be a nobody. He meant for everybody to be somebody. So as one person attains success, so can we all attain success. There is enough success for all; no one is excluded. Success is a wide subject discussion, and there is much more to say than what I have said. I have given you some of the successful attainments of life. I am so pleased to have had your attention. Thank you."[45]

When we have failed, we must appeal to God for help. First John 1:9 (KJV) says, "If we confess our sins, he is faithful and just to forgive us our sins, and to cleanse us from all unrighteousness." Repent of your failures. Stop traveling down the same old road. Change your direction. Accept God's forgiveness and forgive yourself. Don't allow your mistakes to keep you stuck in the mud of yesterday. The old has gone and you have a genesis, a new beginning ahead.

Where there are failure and repentance, there are God's forgiveness and restoration. If there was no failure, we would have no need for God's forgiveness or His help. Our failures will reveal our limitations and dependence on God. God's grace covers all our failures and is able to restore what we may have lost. In Greg Fritz's book *Living with No Regrets*,[46] he states, "if God's plan were for perfect people, He would have never been able to use anybody." Even our mistakes prepare us for the future. Scripture says in Romans 3:23 (KJV), "For all have sinned and come short of the glory of God." And in Proverbs 24:16 (KJV), it says, "For a just man falleth seven times, and riseth up again." You are not a failure because you stumble and fall in life. You become a failure when you fail to get up after the fall.

Our failures are never final for those of us who begin again with God. We can't change our past, but we can make a new start. Jesus died to pay the penalty for *all* our sins, failures, and mistakes. Jesus is our "advocate with our Heavenly Father" (1 John 2:1).

Conclusion

The apostle Paul in his letter to the Philippian church wrote, "I press toward the goal for the prize of the upward call of God in Christ Jesus" (Philippians 3:14 KJV). When he says, "I press toward," he implies progressive movement, moving forward. The idea of upward and onward should be the goal for those who experience failure.

How we reenergize the sad life of slump failures is important to our survival. Jesus invites us to "come to Him all who are weary and heavy-laden and He will give us rest" (paraphrased, Matthew 11:28). Being a Christian does not mean getting a free pass through life or living without making mistakes. However, we must not give up, resign from life, or take an early retirement.

Don't make the Florence Chadwick mistake. Florence was an American swimmer who, in 1952, attempted to swim the chilly ocean waters between Catalina Island and the California shore, which is twenty-six miles. She swam through the fog and choppy seas for fifteen hours. Her muscles began to cramp and her courage weakened. She begged to be taken out of the water, but her mother, riding in the boat beside her, urged her not to give up. Florence became exhausted and stopped swimming. She swam twenty-five and a half miles when she was lifted out of the water and into the boat. Her aides paddled a few more minutes when the fog lifted and Florence discovered that she was less than a half mile from shore. She explained to the waiting news reporters, "All I could see was the fog. I think if I could have seen the shore, I would have made it."[47] The "slump gun" of fog caused Ms. Chadwick to fail, give up, quit when she was close to her goal.

We may fail, but we must not quit. Failure is just a setback. We can always begin again. The Lord is on our side, and in Him we have the victory. No matter what caused your failure or your being knocked down, you don't have to stay down. Get up with a praise on your lips and in your heart. Be like Habakkuk 3:17–19 (KJV).

> "Although the fig tree shall not blossom, neither shall fruit be in the vines; the labour of the olive shall fail, and the fields shall yield no meat; the flock shall be cut off from the fold, and there shall be no herd in the stalls: Yet I will rejoice in the LORD, I will joy in the God of my salvation. The LORD God is my strength, and He will make my feet like hinds' feet, and He will make me to walk upon mine high places."

Encourage yourself in the Lord God Almighty, and get up! Get up in Jesus!

Each day is a fresh start for you to move forward successfully.

Notes

44. Lucado, Max. *Facing Your Giants,* Nashville, TN, Thomas Nelson, Inc., 2007.
45. Draw, Elizabeth L. *Successful Attainment,* Detroit, MI, Family Legacy, 2009.
46. Fritz, Greg. *Living with No Regrets,* Shippensburg, PA, Harrison Publishing House, 2019.
47. Edelson, Paula. *American Women in Sports*, pp. 38–39, New York, NY Facts on File, Inc., 2002.

Don't Look Back

> "No, dear brothers, I am still not all I should be, but I am bringing all my energies to bear on this one thing: Forgetting the past and looking forward to what lies ahead."
> —Philippians 3:13 (KJV)

Have you ever watched someone riding a bike in fast moving traffic? I've noticed that bikers always look behind them for oncoming traffic. Trying to ride a bike or even drive a car while continually looking back can be hazardous to your health. Your focus is distracted, your vision is limited, and you just might develop a crick in your neck. I've often looked back over my life and thought, *"If only I had known what I know now, I would have done a lot of things differently"*. Looking back, I did a lot of foolish and hurtful stuff, and I wish I could retrace my steps, but I can't. Yesterdays are gone forever.

Sir Winston Churchill lets us know that continuous war with our past gives no hope for our future.[48] Looking back can freeze us in our past and keep us from successfully reaching our future. The apostle Paul says in Philippians 3:14 that he's "forgetting the past and looking forward to what lies ahead." Now let me clarify something. We can think about what has happened in our lives, but we must not live or get stuck in the past. When we look back, the tendency is to pick the past apart. We beat up on ourselves with CSW. You know, *coulda, shoulda,* and *woulda* (Ebonics) or correctly stated, *could've, should've* and *would've*. We are good at beating ourselves up with past sins and failures. All this does is waste the present.

Paul tells us to "forget what lies behind." We must not look back in a way that will keep us from forging ahead. Don't look back in a way that makes us prisoners of our past. Looking back in the wrong way enslaves us to past mistakes and sins. Looking back will not allow for the healing of old hurts and painful memories. You can't be useful to the Lord today holding on to yesterday and its mess-ups.

Don't look back; remember back. When you "remember back," you see changes. You see how far you have come and, by the grace of our Lord, where the Lord has brought you from.

God uses our past to help us become the people we are today. He uses our hurts, failures, and mess-ups to strengthen and make us useful for today. We have a testimony to share with others when we "remember back." You can tell others how God has moved in your life, how he brought you through hardships, and when God gave you victories. To remember back is to realize that God is a forgiving, merciful, and loving God. The apostle Paul had many mess-ups and guilt so heavy that he may have given up had he not been aware that God extends new grace and mercy daily. Paul understood that God is faithful to forgive our sins, cleansing us from all unrighteousness when we confess our sins. Paul understood that God would no longer remember our sins. When we confess our sins, failures, mistakes, and mess-ups to God, He forgives and give us a clean slate. With God we can always begin again.

We can't live in the past and still be fully alive. Don't let your yesterdays mess up your today; this will ruin your tomorrow. Don't look back! Instead look to Jesus, the author and finisher of your faith. Look to Jesus, who is able to take your failures and put them behind you. Look to Jesus and His promises, His love, and His guiding light—the light that leads from the shadows of yesterday to the light of tomorrow. Look ahead to the light. We may walk in the shadows, but if we look up, we will see the light. It takes light to make a shadow. A shadow is made by a beam of light that reflects off an object.

Look up! If you walk with your head hung down, you may find a few coins on the ground, but you won't see God's stars shining in the heavens. It takes an upward look and a renewed focus to find the hope and help that God offers. When we focus on God, His sovereign majesty, His glory, and His power, we will have a new outlook and be able to navigate through the shambles of life we have made. We must always allow God's light to shine through our gloomy, dark clouds. Set your eyes toward the hills, where your help comes from. Look to Jesus. He's your strength, your peace, and your blessed hope.

Don't let your past stop you. Trust Jesus and keep on keeping on. Our ability to keep moving forward depends on our trust in God. There comes a time when all we can do is trust Him who is mighty in power, love, grace, and mercy. When we look back and can't see and don't know what's happening, looking forward seems impossible. This is where trusting God pays off. Trusting God makes forward movement possible. Not easy, but possible to accept what we can't see or comprehend. The secret in the trusting is in the doing, putting trusting into practice. We must learn to trust God with every aspect of our lives. As someone who has been through some stuff—serious health issues, deaths of loved ones, broken relationships, no home, and no money (you name it and I've been there)—I've been right in the center or hanging on the edge. As I look back over my life and wonder how I got over, I can tell you it was trusting in God to move me forward. If it had not been for trusting God and knowing that He was on my side, I would still be stuck in the mud of my past.

All too often we focus on our past dark issues and lose sight of the one who can and is able to bring us forward into the light. When we fail to trust God, we have no access to His power, mercy, grace, and help. Our security is in the fact that God never changes and He will *never* leave us. He always knows where we are for; He is omniscient, all knowing.

God is omnipresent. Wherever we are, God is. We have His protection and His provisions for He is omnipotent, all power. We have His forgiveness and eternal life through the precious blood of His Son, Jesus Christ. Don't look back; look forward to progressive movement. In order to reach the end of life's race, look ahead and not back. We have not arrived at our final destination. We will continue to make mistakes as we move ahead. Regardless of our failures, mistakes, and mishaps, we must continue to forge ahead. There is no hope if we continue to look back at past hurts and regrets.

In this earthly life, we are on a racetrack running a race. This race in life is not given to the swift. Running fast, you may get ahead of God and His plans for you. The race is not given to the slow; you may lag behind and miss the opportunities God has for you. Since life's racetrack is not smooth but full of potholes, the race is given to those who endure the falls, to those who get up, wipe themselves off and start again, moving forward according to the steps ordered by God. Looking back, you can't endure because you are constantly rehashing and rehearsing past failures, hurts, and disappointments. To move ahead according to the plans God has for you, you must look and move forward. Dr. Martin Luther King Jr. said it best when he merely stated to his audience, that their best option in any situation is to keep moving forward no matter what method they have to take.[49] Don't look back. Keep on keeping on.

Conclusion

I don't know about you, but I'm taking the lyrics to the hymn below penned by Gabriel and Johnson seriously.

> "I'm pressing on the upward way, new heights I'm gaining every day; still praying as I'm onward bound, Lord, plant my feet on higher ground. My heart has no desire to stay where doubts arise and fears dismay; though some may dwell where those abound, my prayer, my aim, is higher ground. I want to live above the world, though Satan's darts at me are hurled; for faith has caught the joyful sound, the song of saints on higher ground. I want to scale the utmost height and catch a gleam of glory bright; but still I'll pray till heaven I've found, Lord, plant my feet on higher ground."

Refrain: "Lord, lift me up and let me stand, by faith, on Heaven's tableland. A higher plane than I have found; Lord, plant my feet on higher ground."[50]

"I press toward the mark for the prize of the high calling of God in Christ Jesus." -Philippians 3:14 (KJV)

Each day is a fresh start for you to move forward to higher ground.

Notes

48. Sala, Harold J. *Tomorrow Starts Today: February 4th*, Redondo, CA, Barbour Publishing Inc., 2000.
49. King Jr., Martin Luther. *Keep Moving from this Mountain,* Spelman College, Atlanta, GA, 1960, featured in Perseverance Quotes, Persistence Quotes, Martin Luther King Jr. Quotes. https://www.goodreads.com/quotes/26963, 2020.
50. Gabriel, Charles H. and Johnson, Oatman. *Higher Ground,* Chicago, IL, Sweney, Davis, and Entwisle, 1898, now public domain.

Epilogue: Burdens Down

> "Cast thy burden upon the LORD, and he shall sustain thee: he shall never suffer the righteous to be moved."
> —Psalm 55:22 (KJV)

The average brick weighs approximately five pounds. That's not very heavy. The average person, depending on their age, can pick it up easily without any pain or strain. Someone like me, at age eighty-three, might experience some discomfort of bending and rising again. If you took that same five-pound brick, holding it with your hand, your arm extended out to your side, and keeping that position for five to ten minutes, what would be the outcome? I believe it would become very heavy. The longer you held it, the heavier it becomes. Your arm muscles become tired, painful, weighted down, and on the verge of collapsing.

We all have troubles in our lives. There are times when things seem to go against us. First Corinthians 10:13 (KJV) lets us know that. "There hath no temptation (trial) taken you but such as is common to man." In other words, the trials that we experience are the same that everybody will encounter. Jesus said in John 16:33(KJV), "In this world ye shall have tribulation." All of God's children will face the same basic problems. No one is immune. We are all burdened with dysfunctional stuff that serves, seemingly, no constructive purpose but to weigh us down.

As previously discussed in section 4, "My Enemy Is Me: When You Cause the Storm," we have self-induced issues and burdens. Some years ago, while discussing this very problem, my youngest granddaughter wrote a *"Short Word"* for me. She spoke of the times we go through the unnecessary. We get distracted, frustrated, and burdened about life and the things we've brought upon ourselves. We don't listen. We don't feed ourselves with the necessary nourishment—the Word of God—in order to mature and grow. We stunt our growth and block our blessings. Then we have the nerve to blame God and others. We could have prevented all those unhealthy habits and worldly sicknesses that caused us the burden of heartache and pain. We feed ourselves so much junk. Some of us are on a diet from God and His Word. We actually need to gain some weight and become fat in the Lord. It all makes sense to me now and I am so glad that He gives me indispensable food. The food God offers will lighten your burdens, whether self-made or otherwise.[51]

We are encumbered with heavy loads of grief, financial worries, depression, guilt, past hurts, unhealed wounds, unresolved issues, and unforgiveness. We are laden with many problems. We carry burdens we were never meant to carry. Jesus gives us this invitation in Matthew 11:28 (KJV), saying, "Come unto me, all ye that labour and are heavy laden, and I will give you rest." Yet we burden ourselves and have nothing to show for it but bent backs, wrinkled faces, and frustrated souls. We are burdened when we worry, become anxious, and depressed over trials and tribulations. These negative emotions, if we allow them, will seize and strangle us while choking the very life out of us. There are many physical ailments that are associated with worry and being loaded with burdens (headaches, heart palpitations, high blood pressure, weight gain or loss, diarrhea, constipation, and sleep deprivation, to name a few).

In a counseling session, the counselee was asked how she was doing. Her reply was "All right under the circumstances of my burdens." The counselor countered her reply with "What are you doing down there? What are you doing *under* your circumstances, *under* your burden?" Get it? God doesn't want us *under* our burdens or our circumstances. God want us to be overcomers. He tells us to "cast all our cares, anxieties, problems, heavy loads, burdens on Him" (paraphrased, 1 Peter 5:7 KJV).

Allow me to share the thoughts of my eldest grandchildren, Daphne and Mike, on this particular scripture. "According to 1 Peter 5:7, the believers are instructed to cast their cares on God because He cares for us, His children. What does it mean to cast my care upon the Lord, and how is it done? I believe the answer is found in the previous verse, where Peter gives instruction to "humble yourselves therefore under the mighty hand of God" (1 Peter 5:6 KJV). The key word here is "humble." To be humble or to walk in humility means to have an accurate perspective of one's finite ability and insufficiency without God. Many times, we take ownership of issues that produce worry and anxiety that we were never created to carry on our own. God instructs us to cast (or give) our burdens to Him, and not to carry our burdens. The central issue behind this reason of thought is pride, which is expressed by EGO (edging God out). The ministry of reconciliation between God and man is so that we as God's children no longer exist from our own means but we live to the fullest with His help. The greatest act of humility in the believer's life is expressed through prayer. Prayer is humility in action. Prayer allows us to wholeheartedly give our cares to God and submit them under his Lordship. Paul says in Philippians 4 that the shalom, or peace of God, is available to His children. However, the prerequisite is that we must pray and petition God with thanksgiving. Prayer combined with my submission to God's power allows the believer to be "anxious for nothing." Furthermore, verse 8 instructs us to subdue the enemy's lies by focusing on what is pure, praiseworthy, lovely, of good report, etc."[52]

When we walk around with burdens, we are subject to fall beneath the heavy load. We make unwise decisions, seek the wrong avenue of escape, and become prey to Satan and his imps. But I know a man from Galilee who knows your load limit, who is able to carry you and your burdens, and who will keep you from falling. However, this calls for trusting and leaning on Almighty God.

Pastor Emeritus of Pleasant Grove Missionary Baptist Church in Marietta, Georgia, Rev. Benjamin Lockhart, Jr., expresses his thoughts on the keeping power of God with *"Just a Word or Two."* When we fall, we must first lean before we fall. Leaning is between standing and falling. When you start to lean you are not completely down but on your way down. God with His divine power can catch you before you fall. God caught Daniel in the lion's den. God caught Paul on the Damascus Road. God caught Jonah in the belly of a great fish. God can catch you and your heavy burdens before you fall. Jude 24 (KJV) says, "Now unto Him that is able to keep you…" Therefore, we are divinely kept by the grace and mercy of God. He is the keeper of our souls. Our future is in His hands. God cares for us. God is our yesterday, our today, and our tomorrow. God's eye is on the sparrow and He watches over us all."[53]

Psalm 55:22 and 1 Peter 5:7 both begin with the word "Cast." When I hear this word, in the context that it is used in these scriptures, I imagine someone throwing or flinging an object with a quick motion. Picture someone that does a lot of fly fishing. They swing their fishing line behind and cast it forward in front of them with a quick movement of their arm and wrist. Jesus wants us to cast our burdens, to give our burdens to Him with a quickness. Why should we carry them when Jesus is the greatest burden bearer there is and ever will be? We can't look to friends and family to carry our heavy loads. Their backs are bent under their own loads. Give your burdens to Jesus. Come justa casting and give *all* your burdens to Him. Give them to Jesus. Tell Jesus all about your burdens. Why should you carry your burdens by yourself when Jesus is willing and able and offers to share your heavy load? We go to the altar Sunday after Sunday and say we are laying burdens down at the feet of Jesus, and before we can get out the church door, we have them tucked under our arm and are taking them back home with us. Carrying your burdens by yourself shows you don't trust God with your life. It takes humility to admit that you need God. Don't you realize that God loves you? Don't you know that God cares for you and the stuff you go through? Don't you know that when we are at the end of our resources, we are at the beginning of God's never-ending resources?

There is a hymn story that tells of a worried and burdened church member of the late Pastor Charles A. Tindley. She approached Pastor Tindley hoping for a word of comfort. After listening to his parishioner and her concerns, Pastor Tindley replied, "Put all your troubles in a sack, take them to the Lord, and leave them there." This sparked the pastor to write the lyrics to the hymn "Leave It There."[54] This hymn is sung in many churches today. I wonder how many churchgoers notice how the verses of this hymn speak to our troubles and burdens. Look at verse 1 as it addresses financial crisis. "If the world from you with-hold of its silver and its gold, and you have to get along with meager fare. Just remember in His Word, how He feeds the little bird. Take your burden to the Lord and leave it there."

Verse 2 gives insight to our need for healing. "If your body suffers pain and your health you can't regain, and your soul is almost sinking in despair. Jesus knows the pain you feel. He can save and He can heal. Take your burden to the Lord and leave it there."

Verse 3 covers Satan's darts. "When your enemies assail and your heart begins to fail, don't forget that God in heaven answers prayer. He will make a way for you and will lead you safely through. Take your burden to the Lord and leave it there."

Verse 4 has a message for the elderly. "When your youthful days are gone and old age is stealing on, and your body bends beneath the weight of care. He will never leave you then; He'll go with you to the end. Take your burden to the Lord and leave it there."

The refrain/chorus is for any and every burden. It simply says, "Leave it there, leave it there. Take your burden to the Lord and leave it there. If you trust and never doubt, He will surely bring you out. Take your burden to the Lord and leave it there."[55]

God does not want us worried or burdened with problems. They add nothing to our lives. If anything, they take away our peace and joy. Tell Jesus all about your trouble. He will carry you and your burdens. Give God each perplexing problem. Make your cares and concerns known to Him, who is able to keep you from falling under their weight. Lay your burdens down.

My daughter, Sharon, puts it this way in a poem she wrote just for me:

Lay Your Burdens Down

"Do you hold a heavy load? Lay Your Burdens Down. Did you make some bad mistakes? Lay Your Burdens Down. If you fall, surrender all! Lay Your Burdens Down. Caught up in snares, seems no one cares? Lay Your Burdens Down. Feeling mistreated? Feeling defeated? Lay Your Burdens Down. Life can be tough. Enough is Enough! Lay Your Burdens Down. As you pray every day, Lay Your Burdens Down. While you tarry, Jesus will carry. Lay Your Burdens Down. Press On! Bless On! Lay Your Burdens Down. I feel better, so much better since I Laid My Burdens Down!"[56]

When we are burdened down, we need encouragement to rise above our troubles with our heads lifted high. I have a friend who always greets everyone with "Be encouraged." One day I was feeling bad and heavy-laden with troubles. I heard my friend's voice resounding in the atmosphere, saying, "Be encouraged, my sister."

We all need encouraging words. We need them when we're young, we need them when we're old, and we need them in the years in between. It might seem strange, but even those who are seemingly doing well in life need encouragement just to keep them centered and pointed in the right direction. It's clear that those who are struggling need words of encouragement to keep their eyes focused on Jesus. When we are troubled, keeping our minds on Jesus and the Word of God is the best way to stay encouraged. In Him we receive His comfort and His peace that surpasses all understanding. Encouragement and comfort do not come from a cosmic force, a pill, a bottle, or a quick, clever slogan. Our God is the God of all comfort and encouragement.

My sisters and brothers, lay your burdens down. Cry out to Jesus. Psalm 34:17 (KJV) tells us, "The righteous cry, and the LORD heareth, and delivereth them out of all their troubles." At the altar when you kneel to pray, leave your burdens there. All the burdens you've been carrying, leave them at the feet of Jesus and don't you dare pick them up again.

Conclusion

The bottom line is this: when we carry our burdens alone, we have ceased to trust the Lord and that's a sin. Although the calendar says that there are seven days in the week, we only have five. Two of them should never cross our minds when it comes to our burdens of worry. One of them is yesterday that can never be changed. The other is tomorrow for no man holds the future.

Today is the only day we have with Jesus, and with Him all our burdens will be lifted if we only give them to Him. With Jesus we can face anything that comes our way. Remember Philippians 4:13 (KJV). "I can do all things through Christ who strengthens me." Burdens are like a wagon filled with ten-pound bricks. The harder you pull, the weaker you get. The weaker you get, the more apt you are to fall and not have the strength to rise again. Give God your burdens. He is always nearby. He hasn't changed His address. His phone is not disconnected. He's just waiting to hear from you. God is waiting for you to send Him a text, to google Him, or to get on His Facebook page. God will never abandon you. We must always look to God, who is our hope, our deliverer, our peace, and our joy. We must do like it says in Proverbs 3:5 (KJV). "Trust in the Lord with all thine heart and lean not to your own understanding. In all your ways acknowledge Him and He shall direct your paths."

Lay your burdens down. Remember the wrong desires that come into your life aren't anything new and different. Many others have faced exactly the same problems before you. And no temptation is irresistible. You can trust God to keep the temptation from becoming so strong that you can't stand up against it. He has promised to always be with you, never to leave you alone, and He will do what He says. He will show you how to escape temptation's power so that you can bear up patiently against it. You can stand upright if you give your heavy load of burdens to the Lord. My God can do anything but fail. He specializes in lifting heavy burdens, mending broken hearts, and putting the broken pieces of our lives back together again. God is faithful even when our faith slips. Wherever you are on this life's journey, Jehovah Shamma, God is there.

> Dear Father God,
>
> I thank You for being near to all of us who call on You and who call on You in truth. I draw near to You, knowing that You are ever near me and You hear and answer my prayers. Christ Jesus, You healed the sick, opened blinded eyes, caused the deaf to hear, the lame to walk, untied tongues so folk could talk. Come now, Lord, and look upon Your suffering children. Come to their aid. Have mercy upon those in need of financial stability. Release those who walk in fear, anxiety, depression, and guilt.
>
> Father God, many are burdened with problems they have never experienced before and are not sure just what to do. Your word says we can come to You and You will give us rest. Your Word tells us to cast all our cares upon You, and we can do this because You love us.
>
> Today, Lord, I come casting, laying the burdens of those who responded to my survey and those that will read this dissertation. I lay all their burdens at Your feet. I give their burdens to Your tender loving care. Lord, stretch Your mighty hand of hope into every

situation that besets Your children. Move mountains. Calm troubled waters and breathe life into dark dry places. Send Your light to save, restore, and redeem. Send light that heals and protects. Send light that brings joy to sadness. Hold and rescue the silent sufferers. I pray that You speak victory over their lives and victory into their burdens whatever they may be. Grant us all faith to trust You fully. Help us to surrender all of our burdens to You and not take them back again. I pray that this dissertation will encourage and bless each reader. In the precious name of Jesus, the Christ, I believe and I pray. Amen!

Each day is a fresh start for you to move forward in God, in His service, in forgiveness, love, freedom, and victory, in His peace, truth, healing success, and upward to higher ground.

A Note to the Reader

Perhaps I didn't address your particular silent issue; however, I pray that you find encouragement in the midst of your silent suffering to take your issues to the Lord in prayer. Give them all to Jesus. God knows! God sees! God hears! God cares! Let your faith be bigger than your burdens. Go forward, my brothers and sisters, in the strength of the Lord and stand on His promises. It's time to let go and let God.

"Let Go and Let God"

When the clouds seem their darkest and the daylight won't come; When you're up to your ears and drowning and can't find a straw to hang on. When you're faced with life's battles and have no will to fight; Remember: Let go and let God.[57]

If you have not accepted Jesus Christ as your Lord and Savior, I invite you to come to Him by praying this prayer:

> Dear Father God, I confess that I am a sinner. I come in the name of Your Son, Jesus Christ. I repent of my sins. I believe in my heart that He was born, crucified, died, buried, and arose from the grave, all for my salvation and so that I may have eternal life with You. Come into my heart, Lord Jesus, and fill me with the Holy Spirit. Thank You, God, for Your grace, mercy, love, and my salvation. In the name of Jesus, I pray. Amen.

Each day is a fresh start for you to move forward saved in Jesus's name.

Notes

51. Fordham, Delphine L. *A Short Word,* Powder Springs, GA, Family Legacy, 2018.
52. Morrison, Mike and Daphne. *Thoughts on 1 Peter 5:7,* Lithia Springs, GA, Family Legacy, 2021.
53. Lockhart Jr., Benjamin. *Just a Word or Two,* Marietta, GA, Family Legacy, 2021.
54. Osbeck, Kenneth W. *101 Hymn Stories,* p. 171, Grand Rapids, MI, Kregal Publications. 1985.
55. Tindley, Charles A. "Leave It There", Philadelphia, PA, Hope Publishing Co., 1916, public domain.
56. Fordham, Sharon D. *Lay Your Burdens Down,* Dallas, GA, Family Legacy, 2021.
57. Lewis, Pamilla deLeon. *Let Go and Let God,* New York, NY, https:/www.authorsden.com, 2003.

Appendix A

Letter of Invitation to Survey Group

September 24, 2021

My Dear Brothers and Sisters in Christ,

As a doctoral student at Christian Bible College, I am required to write a dissertation. My proposed subject centers around God's servants who suffer in silence due to the weight of excess baggage that they continue to carry in their lives. I am inviting you to participate in the preparation of my dissertation. The data collected will provide useful information regarding issues suffered in silence that will be addressed first by God's Word and second through my personal life experiences.

The questionnaire will require approximately five to ten minutes to complete. There is no compensation for responding. It is strictly voluntary, and there is no known risk. In order to ensure the confidentiality and anonymity of the survey, *do not* use your name, address, phone number, or any other means of identification. Please use the enclosed self-addressed envelope provided for mailing the survey, and return it no later than October 28, 2021, as time is important. Thank you for your prayers and your help.

Sincerely,

_____
Rev. LaRuth E. Lockhart

Enclosure: Doctoral Survey "Suffering in Silence"

Appendix B

Survey Questionnaire/ Information Gathering

"Suffering in Silence" Doctoral Survey

"Examine yourselves to see whether you are in the faith; test yourselves." -2 Corinthians 13:5 (KJV)

Please check all that apply.

Gender: ____male ____female

1. Age bracket: __(21–30) __(31–40) __(41–50) __(51–60) __(60 +)

2. Marital status: __single __married __divorced __separated __widowed

3. Length of church membership: ____(1–3 yrs.) ____(3–5 yrs.) ____(5–10 yrs.) ____(10–15 yrs.) ____(15 + yrs.)

4. Do you believe in God and His Word? ____Yes ____No ____Unsure

5. Ministerial status: _____licensed minister _____ordained minister _____elder _____deacon _____ministerial/leadership other: _____

6. Past/present church ministries: _____Bible study _____Sunday school _____choir _____children/teen _____usher _____bereavement _____benevolent _____finance _____Prayer band other: _____

   But remember this—the wrong desires that come into your life aren't anything new and different. (1 Corinthians 10:13 TLB)

7. What is your silent suffering issue? _____
   _____

8. What have you done about it? _____
   _____

9. What was the outcome/results? _____
   _____

Additional comments: _____
_____

Appendix C

Survey Results

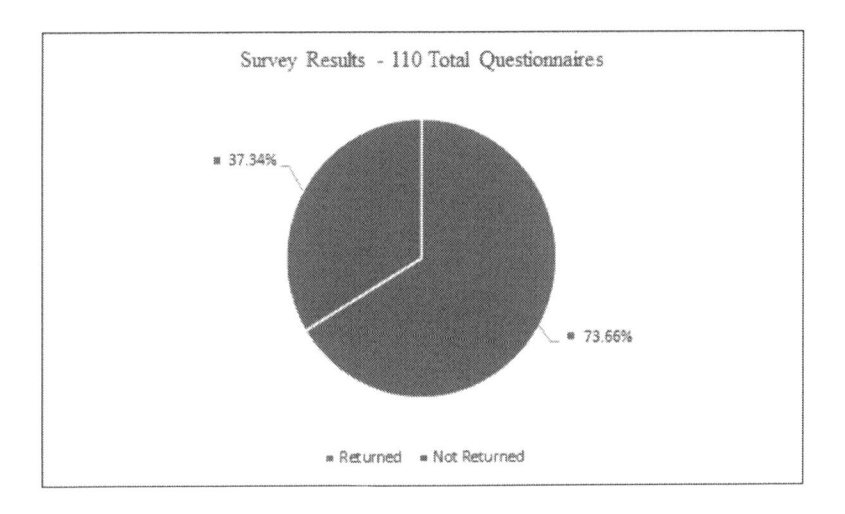

Survey Results - 110 Total Questionnaires

- 37.34% Returned
- 73.66% Not Returned

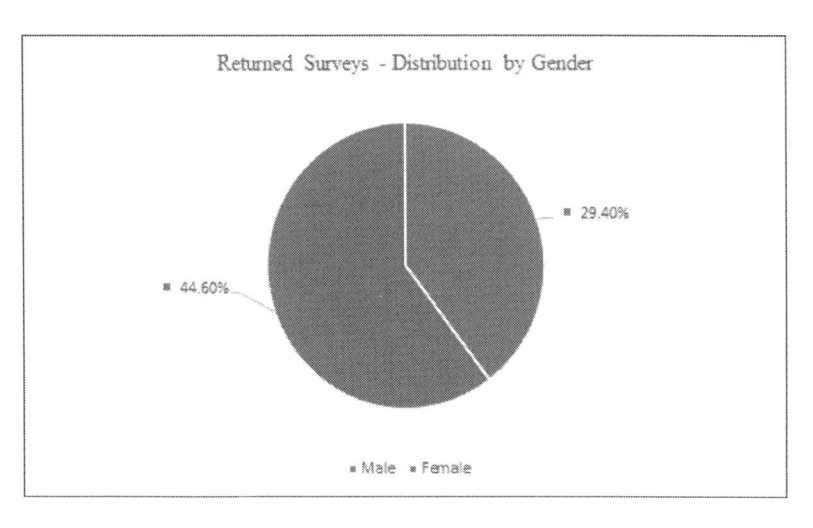

Returned Surveys - Distribution by Gender

- 29.40%
- 44.60%

■ Male ■ Female

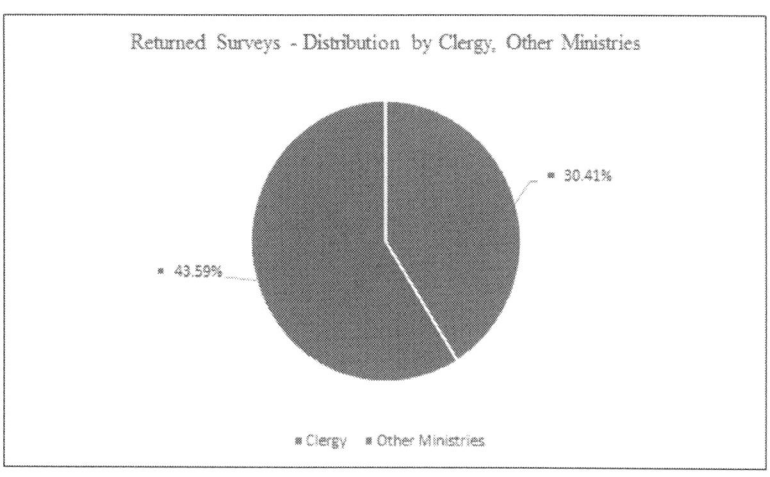

Returned Surveys - Distribution by Clergy, Other Ministries

- 30.41%
- 43.59%

■ Clergy ■ Other Ministries

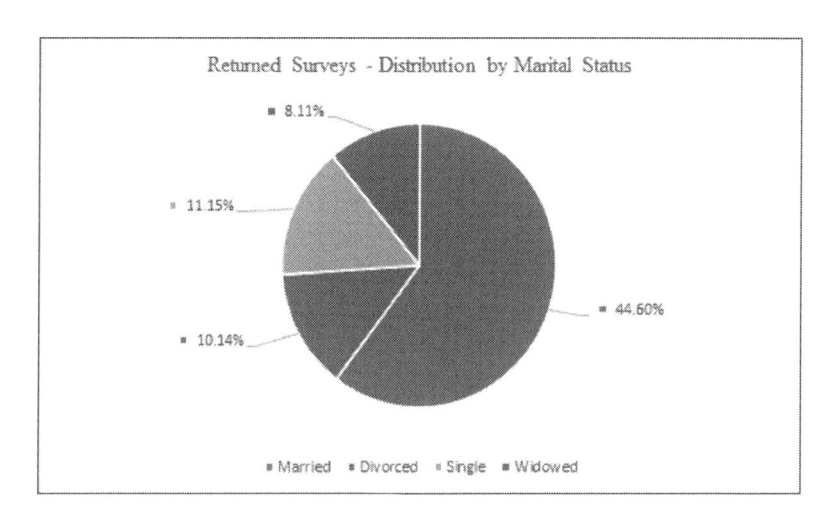

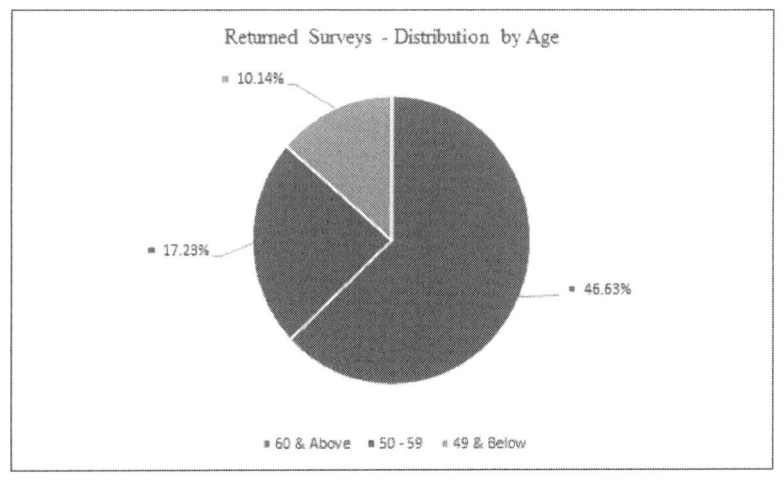

Returned Surveys - Distribution by Marital Status

- 44.60% Married
- 10.14% Divorced
- 11.15% Single
- 8.11% Widowed

Returned Surveys - Distribution by Age

- 46.63% 49 & Below
- 17.23% 50 - 59
- 10.14% 60 & Above

Geographic Areas

Arizona, Florida, Georgia, Michigan, Ohio, and Texas.

Areas of Concern

Denial, sexual abuse, unforgiveness, internal conflict, grief and loss, health issues, moving from failure to success, worry and stress, bitterness and anger.

Complete Notes

1. Broger, John C. *Self-Confrontation: A Manual for In-Depth Discipleship,* CA, Biblical Counseling Foundation (BFC), 1991.
2. Unknown. The Holy Bible (KJV), Hebrews 12:1, Nashville, TN, Broadman and Holman, 1996.
3. Fisher, James, MD. Office visit, patient-physician conversation, Marietta, GA, Fisher-Lockhart, 2021.
4. Apostle Paul. The Holy Bible (KJV), 2 Corinthians 1:3–4, Nashville, TN, Broadman and Holman, 1996.
5. Wikipedians. "The History of Masks," Wikipedia: The Free Encyclopedia, Wikimedia Foundation, last edited 2021.
6. Parfieneuk, I. and Stawinski, S. J. *Glosbe English-Latin Dictionary,* Poland, World Wide Webb, 2011.
7. Sparks, Susan. "The Masks That We Wear," *Psychology Today,* New York City, James Thomas, October 20, 2015.
8. Dunbar, Paul Laurence. "We Wear the Mask," *The Complete Poems of Paul Laurence Dunbar,* New York, Dodd, Mead and Company, 1896, public domain.
9. Matthew. The Holy Bible (KJV), Matthew 7:3–4, Nashville, TN, Broadman and Holman, 1996.
10. Guest, Edgar A. *Myself,* Detroit, MI, Detroit Free Press, 1998, public domain, 1919.
11. Apostle Paul. The Holy Bible (KJV), Romans 12:2–3, Nashville, TN, Broadman and Holman, 1996.
12. Langberg, Diane. "Shattered Innocence: Childhood Sexual Abuse," Forest, VA, *Christian Counseling Today,* vol. 23, no. 1, 2015.

13. Abel, Gene. *Abel Assessment of Sexual Interest,* Atlanta, GA, https://www.childmolestationprevention.org/pdfs/study.pdf, 1980.
14. Hall, M. and Hall, J. *The Long-Term Effects of Childhood Sexual Abuse,* Alexandria, VA, American Counseling Association, 2017.
15. Loyola Education Department. *Common Reactions to Sexual Assault,* Baltimore, MD, Loyola University Counseling Center, 2021.
16. Akulikowski. *Common Victim Behaviors of Survivors of Sexual Abuse,* PA, Pennsylvania Coalition Against Rape (PCARP), 2013.
17. Jefferson. LaRuth. *The Old Woman's Problem,* Southfield, MI, Biblical Counseling, Self-Confrontation (BC-1), 1998.
18. Lawrenz, Mel. *How Forgiveness Works,* Brookfield, WI, http://www.preching.com, 2010.
19. Apostle Paul. The Holy Bible (KJV), Galatians 4:4–6, Nashville, TN, Broadman and Holman, 1996.
20. Unknown. Our Daily Bread, October 19, Grand Rapids, MI, Discovery House Publishers Ministries, 1999.
21. Lewis, C. S. *Mere Christianity,* p.115, New York City, Touchstone Books, 1996.
22. May-Watson, Barbara A. "Forgiveness: Get in the Game." Southfield, MI, by permission Barbara's son, Wayne Watson, 2021.
23. King Jr., Martin Luther. *The Meaning of Forgiveness,* Stanford, CA, Research Education Institute @ Stanford.Edu., 1954.
24. Apostle Paul. "On Love," 1 Corinthians 13:4–8 (KJV), Nashville, TN, Broadman and Holman, 1996.
25. King Jr., Martin Luther. *Loving Your Enemies,* Montgomery, AL, http://www.kinginstitute.standford.edu/king-papers, 1957.
26. Evans, Tony. *Book of Illustrations: Love,* p. 196, Chicago, IL, Moody Publishers, 2009.
27. Holtz, Albert. *Pilgrim Road: A Benedictine Journey through Lent,* Harrisburg, PA, Morehouse Publishing, 2006.
28. Davis, Malisa. *Break These Chains,* San Jose, CA, https://allpoetry.com/poem/6806207-Break-These-Chains-by-malisa101664, 2010.
29. Hawkins, Walter. "There's a War Going On," *Love Alive III,* Waco, TX, Light Records, Word Records-MNRK Music Group, 1993.

30. Luther, Martin. *The Westminster Confession of Faith,* "Of Good Works," *chapter XVI, v, vi.* London-Edinburg, England, Evan Tyler, printer King M.E.M., 1646–1647.
31. Kleinhans, Kathryn, A. *Saints and Sinners,* Columbus, OH, https://www.livinglutheran.org.saints-sinners, 2005.
32. Writer, Staff. *What Causes Storms,* Oakland, CA, https://www.reference.com/askmediagroup, 2000.
33. Mullins, Margaret Christine. *When the Storms of Life Are Ragging,* Freeport, FL, https://www.authorsden.com/, 2009.
34. Pope, Alexander. *An Essay on Criticism, Part 2,* London, EN, https://www.phrases.org.UK, Kessinger Publishing, 2004 (first published 1711).
35. Wilson, Clerow "Flip" Jr. *The Devil Made Me Buy This Dress Album,* New York, https://en.Wikipedia.org/the_flip_wilson_show, Little David Records, NBC, 1979.
36. Harper, Donnie, New Jersey Mass Choir. *Hope of the World*: *It's in Jesus.* Pittsburgh, https://www.hoperecords.com, Hope Records, 1992.
37. Kübler-Ross, Elisabeth. *Death and Dying,* New York City, NY, Macmillan Publishing Co., 1969.
38. Wiersbe, Warren W. and Wiersbe, David W. *Comforting the Bereaved*, Chicago, IL, Moody Press, 1985.
39. Wolfelt, Alan D. *The Journey through Grief: Reflections on Healing,* Fort Collins, CO, Center for Loss and Life Transition, Companion Press, 1997.
40. Wolterstorff, Nicholas. *Lament for a Son,* p. 92, Grand Rapids, MI, William B. Eerdmans Publishing Co., 1987.
41. Siegel, Bernie S. *Love, Medicine and Miracles.* New York City, NY, Harper and Row Publishers, 1986.
42. Shmerling, Robert H. *Top Ten Causes of Death,* Boston, MA, Harvard Publishing, Harvard Medical School, 2016.
43. Jefferson, LaRuth E. *Goodbye, My Love: Recipes for Hope,* Detroit, MI, Sprint PCS, 2000.
44. Lucado, Max. *Facing Your Giants,* Nashville, TN, Thomas Nelson, Inc., 2007.

45. Draw, Elizabeth L. *Successful Attainment,* Detroit, MI, Family Legacy, 2009.
46. Fritz, Greg. *Living with No Regrets,* Shippensburg, PA, Harrison Publishing House, 2019.
47. Edelson, Paula. *American Women in Sports,* pp. 38–39, New York, NY Facts on File, Inc., 2002.
48. Sala, Harold J. *Tomorrow Starts Today: February 4th,* Redondo, CA, Barbour Publishing Inc., 2000.
49. King Jr., Martin Luther. *Keep Moving from This Mountain,* Spelman College, 1960, Atlanta, GA, featured in Perseverance Quotes, Persistence Quotes, Martin Luther King Quotes https://www.goodreads.com/quotes/26963, 2020.
50. Gabriel, Charles H. and Johnson, Oatman. *Higher Ground,* Chicago, IL, Sweney, Davis, and Entwisle, 1898, now public domain.
51. Fordham, Delphine L. *A Short Word.* Powder Springs, GA, Family Legacy, 2018.
52. Morrison, Mike and Daphne. *Thoughts on 1 Peter 5:7,* Lithia Springs, GA, Family Legacy, 2021.
53. Lockhart Jr., Benjamin. *Just a Word or Two*, Marietta, GA, Family Legacy, 2021.
54. Osbeck, Kenneth W. *101 Hymn Stories,* p. 171, Grand Rapids, MI, Kregal Publications, 1985.
55. Tindley, Charles A. "Leave It There", Philadelphia, PA, Hope Publishing Co., 1916, public domain.
56. Fordham, Sharon D. *Lay Your Burdens Down,* Dallas, GA, Family Legacy, 2021.
57. Lewis, Pamilla deLeon, *Let Go and Let God,* New York, NY, https:/www.authorsden.com., 2003.

Bibliography

Abel, Gene. *Abel Assessment of Sexual Interest,* Atlanta, GA, https://www.childmolestationprevention.org/pdfs/study.pdf, 1980.

Akulikowski. *Common Victim Behaviors of Survivors of Sexual Abuse,* PA, Pennsylvania Coalition Against Rape (PCARP), 2013.

Broger, John C. *Self-Confrontation: A Manual for In-Depth Discipleship,* CA, Biblical Counseling Foundation (BFC), 1991.

Davis, Malisa. *Break These Chains.* San Jose, CA, https://allpoetry.com/poem/6806207-Break-These-Chains-by-malisa101664, 2010.

Dunbar, Paul Laurence. "We Wear the Mask," *The Complete Poems of Paul Laurence Dunbar,* New York, Dodd, Mead and Company, 1896, public domain.

Draw, Elizabeth L. *Successful Attainment,* Detroit, MI, Family Legacy, 2009.

Edelson, Paula. *American Women in Sports,* pp. 38–39, New York, NY Facts on File, Inc., 2002.

Evans, Tony. *Book of Illustrations: Love,* p. 196, Chicago, IL, Moody Publishers, 2009.

Fisher, James, MD. Office visit, patient-physician conversation, Marietta, GA, Fisher-Lockhart, 2021.

Fordham, Delphine L. *A Short Word,* Powder Springs, GA, Family Legacy, 2018.

Fordham, Sharon D. *Lay Your Burdens Down,* Dallas, GA, Family Legacy, 2021.

Fritz, Greg. *Living with No Regrets.* Shippensburg, PA, Harrison Publishing House. 2019.

Guest, Edgar A. *Myself.* Detroit, MI, Detroit Free Press, 1998, public domain, 1919.

Gabriel, Charles H. and Johnson, Oatman. *Higher Ground,* Chicago, IL, Sweney, Davis, and Entwisle, 1898, now public domain.

Hall, M. and Hall, J. *The Long-Term Effects of Childhood Sexual Abuse,* Alexandria, VA, American Counseling Association, 2017.

Harper, Donnie, New Jersey Mass Choir. *Hope of the World*: *It's in Jesus*, Pittsburgh, https://www.hoperecords.com, Hope Records, 1992.

Hawkins, Walter. "There's a War Going On," *Love Alive III,* Waco, TX, Light Records, Word Records-MNRK Music Group, 1993.

Holtz, Albert. *Pilgrim Road: A Benedictine Journey through Lent*, Harrisburg, PA, Morehouse Publishing, 2006.

Jefferson. LaRuth. *The Old Woman's Problem,* Southfield, MI, Biblical Counseling, Self-Confrontation (BC-1), 1998.

Jefferson, LaRuth E. *Goodbye, My Love: Recipes for Hope,* Detroit, MI, Sprint PCS, 2000.

King Jr., Martin Luther. *The Meaning of Forgiveness,* Stanford, CA, Research Education Institute @ Stanford.Edu., 1954.

King Jr., Martin Luther. *Loving Your Enemies,* Montgomery, AL, http://www.kinginstitute.standford.edu/king-papers, 1957.

King Jr., Martin, Luther. *Keep Moving from This Mountain,* Spelman College, 1960, Atlanta, GA, featured in Perseverance Quotes, Persistence Quotes, Martin Luther King Quotes https://www.goodreads.com/quotes/26963, 2020.

Kleinhans, Kathryn, A. *Saints and Sinners,* Columbus, OH, https://www.livinglutheran.org./saints-sinners, 2005.

Kübler-Ross, Elisabeth. *Death and Dying,* New York City, NY, Macmillan Publishing Co., 1969.

Langberg, Diane. "Shattered Innocence: Childhood Sexual Abuse," Forest, VA, *Christian Counseling Today,* vol. 23, no. 1, 2015.

Lawrenz, Mel. *How Forgiveness Works,* Brookfield, WI, http://www.preching.com, 2010.

Lewis, C. S. *Mere Christianity,* p. 115, New York City, Touchstone Books, 1996.

Lockhart Jr., Benjamin. *Just a Word or Two*, Marietta, GA, Family Legacy, 2021.

Loyola Education Department. *Common Reactions to Sexual Assault,* Baltimore, MD, Loyola University Counseling Center, 2021.

Lucado, Max. *Facing Your Giants,* Nashville, TN, Thomas Nelson, Inc., 2007.

Luther, Martin. *The Westminster Confession of Faith,* "Of Good Works," chapter XVI, v, vi. London-Edinburg, England, Evan Tyler, printer King M.E.M., 1646–1647.

Matthew. The Holy Bible (KJV), Matthew 7:3–4, Nashville, TN, Broadman and Holman, 1996.

May-Watson, Barbara A. "Forgiveness: Get in the Game," Southfield, MI, by permission Barbara's son, Wayne Watson, 2021.

Morrison, Mike and Daphne. *Thoughts on 1 Peter 5:7,* Lithia Springs, GA, Legacy, 2021.

Mullins, Margaret Christine. *When the Storms of Life Are Ragging,* Freeport, FL, https://www.authorsden.com/, 2009.

Osbeck, Kenneth W. *101 Hymn Stories,* p. 171, Grand Rapids, MI, Kregal Publications, 1985.

Parfieneuk, I. and Stawinski, S. J. *Glosbe English-Latin Dictionary,* Poland, World Wide Web, 2011.

Apostle Paul. The Holy Bible (KJV), 2 Corinthians 1:3–4, Nashville, TN, Broadman and Holman, 1996.

Apostle Paul. The Holy Bible (KJV), Romans 12:2–3, Nashville, TN, Broadman and Holman, 1996.

Apostle Paul. The Holy Bible (KJV), Galatians 4:4–6, Nashville, TN, Broadman and Holman, 1996.

Apostle Paul. "On Love," 1 Corinthians 13:4–8 (KJV), Nashville, TN, Broadman and Holman, 1996.

Pope, Alexander. *An Essay on Criticism, Part 2,* London, EN, https://www.phrases.org.UK, Kessinger Publishing, 2004 (first published 1711).

Sala, Harold J. *Tomorrow Starts Today: February 4th,*. Redondo, CA, Barbour Publishing Inc., 2000.

Siegel, Bernie S. *Love, Medicine and Miracles,* New York City, NY, Harper and Row Publishers, 1986.

Shmerling, Robert H. *Top Ten Causes of Death,* Boston, MA, Harvard Publishing, Harvard Medical School, 2016.

Sparks, Susan. "The Masks That We Wear" *Psychology Today,* New York City, James Thomas, October 20, 2015.

Staff writer. *What Causes Storms.* Oakland, CA, https://www.reference.com/askmediagroup, 2000.

Tindley, Charles A. *Leave It There,* Philadelphia, PA, Hope Publishing Co., 1916, public domain.

Unknown. The Holy Bible (KJV), Hebrews 12:1, Nashville, TN, Broadman and Holman, 1996.

Unknown. Our Daily Bread, October 19, Grand Rapids, MI, Discovery House Publishers Ministries, 1999.

Wikipedians. "The History of Masks," Wikipedia: The Free Encyclopedia, Wikimedia Foundation, last edited 2021.

Wiersbe, Warren W. and Wiersbe, David W. *Comforting the Bereaved*, Chicago, IL, Moody Press, 1985.

Wilson, Clerow "Flip" Jr. *The Devil Made Me Buy This Dress Album,* New York, https://en.Wikipedia.org/the_flip_wilson_show, Little David Records, NBC, 1979.

Wolfelt, Alan D. *The Journey through Grief: Reflections on Healing,* Fort Collins, CO, Center for Loss and Life Transition, Companion Press, 1997.

Wolterstorff, Nicholas. *Lament for a Son,* p. 92, Grand Rapids, MI, William B. Eerdmans Publishing Co., 1987.

Made in the USA
Columbia, SC
28 September 2024